THE FOUR WAYS OF DIVORCE

A Concise Guide to

What You Need To Know

About Divorce

Using

Litigation

Negotiation

Collaboration

and

Mediation

So You Don't Pay More Than You Should

Rachel L. Virk

Vanguard Books, LLC

D1502399

Published by Vanguard Books, LLC
46090 Lake Center Plaza, Suite 307
Potomac Falls, VA 20165-5879
703-444-6604

Additional copies may be obtained from:

www.thefourwaysofdivorce.com

*

Or from Rachel L. Virk, P.C. www.virk-law.com 703.444.3355

*

Or Contact Vanguard Books, LLC 703.444.6604

*

Also available at www.amazon.com

ABOUT THE AUTHOR

Rachel L. Virk, President of Rachel L. Virk, P.C., has been in practice since 1989, litigating, negotiating, collaborating and mediating divorce cases in Northern Virginia.

She is Certified as a Mediator by the Virginia Supreme Court at the Circuit Court Family level, and is a trained Collaborative Law Practitioner.

TABLE OF CONTENTS

This article is reprinted from when it first appeared in the fall 2008 issue of Family Law News published by the Family Law Section of the Virginia State Bar Association.

ACKNOWLEDGEMENTS

I would like to express my sincere appreciation to all those who provided their time and energy in support of the creation of this book. Some offered to provide assistance, some were asked and all were willing. Any imperfections in the work are probably due to sound advice which I did not follow, and in no way reflect the thoughts of those who provided input to me. There are other individuals not mentioned below, who also provided encouragement along the way. My thanks go out to each of you for your enthusiasm and support.

Richard "Dick" Byrd, Esquire, a giant in the Virginia and Northern Virginia family law communities, made numerous clarifying edits to an early draft manuscript. Sorry I didn't answer all of the questions the book poses – that would be another book in itself!

Kathy Carroll, my paralegal and friend, transcribed every initial chapter of this book, and has been instrumental in the development and continuation of my family law practice.

Steve Coffee, webmaster, at www.chaosabatement.com. No sense in writing a book if no one looks at it. Thanks for all the help with the cover design and website. I love working with you. Maybe some day we'll meet and I'll see what you look like.

Stanley B. Corey, Jr., CFP, ChFC, has been of great assistance to me in "figuring out the numbers" in my litigation, negotiation, collaboration and mediation practices over the years, and offered helpful suggestions from his review of a draft manuscript.

Larry Gaughan, Esquire, a pioneer in the Virginia mediation community, kindly allowed for my inclusion of the forms *he* created in Appendix 2 of this book.

Samuel Jackson, Esquire, a tall figure in the Virginia Alternative Dispute Resolution community, offered to take a look at an early draft manuscript, and provided insights which led to further clarifications of the work.

My sister, Deborah Lennington, read the earliest version of this book, and provided redirection. Accordingly, this version looks nothing like that one.

Beth Spring, Licensed Marriage and Family Therapist, sharpened her red editing pencils, and read a draft of the manuscript not once, but twice. Incorporating those red changes you sat and discussed with me has helped to make the book better.

Pamela K. Squires, Paralegal and Retirement Benefits Specialist, provided and continues to provide to me her dizzying in-depth understanding of the ins and outs of government, military and private retirement benefits.

Brigadier General Manmohan Singh Virk, (Retired), who offered to review the manuscript, provided the insight of one to whom the whole concept of divorce is unfathomable, and made numerous helpful suggestions and corrections from a very careful reading of each word. I am still conflicted over the use of "can not" and "cannot."

My husband Vijay, and our two young children, spent many Saturdays without Mommy, as I sat in my office working on this book and looking at their pictures. I'm glad it is done.

My deepest gratitude goes to those thousands of individuals whom I have been honored to assist as their marriages ended. Their struggles and triumphs provide the inspiration for this book. It has been and remains my privilege to try to help those going through this tumultuous time, and it is my hope that this book will provide some assistance in that process.

Rachel Virk
Potomac Falls, Virginia
January, 2009

DEDICATION

To the Prince Charming

my grandmother always told me

would ride up to me on his horse.

Thank you for making it all happen.

And to my children,

the arrows we send off to a future

we will someday see only from above.

DISCLAIMER

This book is only intended to provide general information, and does not constitute legal advice. The laws of each state vary, and each marital situation is unique. You should seek the assistance of an attorney on your own behalf before taking action.

PREFACE

A person can be defined by what he or she loves most. As you go through your divorce, you and your spouse will each show yourselves, each other, your families, your communities and the world what means most to each of you. You may choose to place the most priority upon personal comfort, earthly pleasures, revenge for perceived injustices, appearances, money, principles, or upon other individuals such as your children or the new love of your life.

If you discover that your attractive face is merely masking an ugly heart or soul, and if that matters to you, your divorce will provide you with the opportunity to readjust your priorities. You will be given the chance to work towards self-improvement as you create your new life, and if you have children, the new life for your two-home family.

If you discover that it is high time you addressed the inner demons which sabotage your relationships, your divorce will provide you with the opportunity to identify those demons and turn on the light which can chase them away. Healthy relationships and failed relationships are the mirrors which show us who we truly are.

If you discover that you really were not born simply for the purpose of being abused, your divorce will provide you with the opportunity to seek the help you need to identify abuse, and to shut it down. You may even come to the realization that if you are tolerating the abuse of your children, you may be just as guilty of abusing them as is the abuser, and that if you have children who are watching abuse in your marriage, you are teaching them that abuse is acceptable.

You may need to journey down the warpath to finally stand up for what you must. Or if you and your X2B don't hate each other just because you are getting a divorce, you may work together to custom design your new separate lives, or your restructured family. Whichever path you take, whether adversarial or nonadversarial, this book will guide you on your travels, and will point out for you what you need to think about and look at along the way.

INTRODUCTION

Your life is moving along, and <u>WHAM</u>. Out of the blue, your marriage is in trouble. Or perhaps even though you knew it was coming for quite some time, things have finally gotten to "that point." You are heading for a divorce.

You are confused, worried, hurt, angry, ashamed, scared and in turmoil.

How can you tell everyone?

What should you do?

You have the ability to control the direction your life will take, and to make things work out for you. You also have the ability to let your spouse and circumstances spiral your life out of control.

Your journey through the divorce process will follow either a litigation, negotiation, collaboration or mediation path. You need to understand these four options in order to stay on the path that will lead you to where you want to be.

The Four Ways of Divorce takes you through the progression of emotions you will experience as you go through your divorce, describes the various options available to obtain a resolution of your concerns, provides information as to how to select a legal professional to help you resolve your divorce, and explains why you may wish to utilize the services of other professionals in the divorce field.

The Four Ways of Divorce also tells you what needs to be decided upon between you and your spouse, sets forth what you need to find out about in order to make informed decisions, touches upon tax considerations and considerations involving members of the military, and addresses the impact of divorce on children.

The Four Ways of Divorce then clarifies how you can embody your decisions in a legally binding document, or what will happen if you "go to court."

The back of the book contains a chart for the easy comparison of the litigation, negotiation, collaboration and mediation processes, along with many helpful financial worksheets for your use. You will also find a description of the Informative Mediation Process, and an extremely useful General List of Topics to be Resolved by your divorce.

So grab a highlighter or a pen, and mark up those questions and points applicable to your current situation in the pages that follow.

Don't avoid dealing with the breakup of your marriage, or you may lose control over your life. If you keep turning your back on reality, eventually it will kick you in the butt. Seek out the proper professional to inform and advise you, based on your unique situation and under your state's current laws. Learn by using this book how you, with that professional, can manage and control the divorce process, to create the best possible future for you and for your family.

Chapter One

I'M HEADING FOR A DIVORCE –
WHAT SHOULD I DO,
WHERE DO I START?

You want out. You no longer love or need your spouse. The kids are older, and you are now earning a living wage. You are tired of your spouse's drinking, untreated mental instability, abusiveness or emotional problems manifested in part by destructive spending habits or other addictions.

Or your spouse has informed you that he or she wants a divorce, or no longer loves you. You find the cell phone records, emails, credit card receipts, hotel records or cards to your spouse from his or her paramour.

You decide that if your spouse is unable to make you feel loved, fulfilled and happy, there may be someone else out there who can. You don't want to feel empty and sad all the time anymore.

You finally found your soul mate, and it is not your spouse.

Now what?

IF YOU ARE THE ONE WHO WANTS OUT . . .

Be fair. Be honest. Come clean. Accept the consequences of your decision – all of the consequences. Stop trying to have one foot in each of two doors. Either stay put, or walk through the other door. Deal with it. Some amount of "yes, no, maybe, I don't know" is to be expected, but at some point you must make a decision to either leave or to stay.

You may want to end the marriage, but don't really want to hurt your spouse. You may believe that you are somehow hurting your spouse less by breaking it to him or her gradually over time. So you may think it better to talk of "wanting to separate" because you "need some space," instead of using the "D" for "Divorce" word.

However, if you tell your spouse that you are *thinking* of divorce, and don't clearly and definitely say that you *want* a D-I-V-O-R-C-E, you are in effect telling your spouse that there is a one in a million chance you could reconcile. If you tell your spouse, who doesn't want the marriage to end, that there is a one in a million chance that the marriage won't end, what do you think your spouse is hearing? He or she is hearing you say, "There is a . . . chance the marriage won't end." People enthusiastically buy lottery tickets with lower chances of winning than that.

You will have to face the fact that you WILL hurt your spouse by saying that you want out, and you must then clearly tell him or her that the marriage is over. If you instead tell your spouse that you don't want a divorce, but that you only "need some time to sort things out," you are quite possibly being selfish and unfair to your spouse. You will paralyze your spouse, holding him or her back from accepting the end of the marriage, and from making his or her own plan for the future.

You may believe your spouse would be so angry if you say you truly want a D-I-V-O-R-C-E, that he or she would make your life even more difficult, or would hurt the children just to hurt you. Some angry people feel justified in trying to hurt back the people who cause them pain.

Anger is not created in a vacuum. Some choose, either consciously or subconsciously, not to feel pain, fear, shame or frustration. They will instead mask those feelings, and then turn them into anger. Many angry people are angry because they have been hurt, and still carry around unresolved pain inflicted upon them in the past, or in childhood, which pain was never faced or addressed.

If your spouse is an angry person, and you will be causing him or her even more pain by leaving the marriage, prolonging the process may just prolong the conflict. So get it over with. If your spouse is not a danger to you, you may create pain to your spouse (and therefore anger directed at you) for a shorter period of time, by being honest early on about wanting to end the marriage. If, however, your spouse is a violent person, you will need a plan, and will need help in letting your spouse know the marriage is over, in order to stay safe.

Perhaps you want out, but only if everything can work out for you. You may want to know the light is still on for you at home with your spouse if you lose your job, or if the new love interest doesn't marry you after all. If you have a financially comfortable married life, and are afraid you won't have a fallback if you are divorced and then lose your job, welcome to the real world. There are no guarantees in life. Again, it isn't fair to everyone to make them put their lives on hold and to be hurt by you, while you see if you can make a go of it on your own. Either stay or leave.

IF YOU ARE THE ONE WHO IS BEING LEFT...

You will probably journey back and forth through the following stages as part of the normal process:

STAGE 1 – DENIAL / AVOIDANCE

If I bury my head in the sand, the problem will go away. I'm used to this. It'll blow over like it always does. I have no options anyway, and can't afford to leave. This is just my lot in life. My happiness isn't meant to be.

My family would disapprove of a divorce. There is a social stigma to divorce. My family's honor is at stake both here and in our home country. If I get a divorce, everyone will say that I could not make my marriage work. If I get a divorce I am a failure. Divorce is against my religious beliefs. My suffering is my cross to bear.

My spouse doesn't really mean it, and would *never* actually leave me. My spouse will change. I will change. It's springtime now, and I'm feeling better. It's not always that bad. Maybe things will improve. I'll stay a bit longer for the sake of the children. I don't want to ruin the holidays.

My spouse would *never* cheat on me. It'll all work out. I'll keep pretending nothing's wrong until I convince myself that I'm not dying just a little more every day.

Then, once you can no longer look reality right in the face and continue to deny it, you will move to…

STAGE 2 – BARGAINING

Maybe we can both find happiness, if only …

If only the drinking would stop, or if my spouse would get on or stay on his or her medication. If we could just go to counseling together, or to AA, we could work out all of our problems. If we could get the finances under control, things would be better. If only we could move away from the paramour, or if there were a job change, our worries would end. If only we had more time together, and my spouse paid more attention to me and to the kids, we'd all be happier. Or if a better or higher paying job would come along. Or if the in-laws would stop interfering. All of our problems could be fixed if only … if only …

The magical wishful thinking is not solving anything. You are simply trying to rearrange the furniture on the deck of a sinking ship. You are now heading right into …

STAGE 3 – GRIEF/ FEAR/ SHOCK/ CONFUSION/ TURMOIL

It's getting harder to live this way. There are more bad days than good. The children are really suffering. They are acting out, their grades are falling and they're learning all the wrong things from this dysfunctional marriage. The tension at home is so thick no one can breathe. Everyone is walking on eggshells. I don't know who I really am anymore.

Why did this have to happen? Life is not fair. Why me? What will I do? How can I afford to live if there is a divorce? How will the children deal with a divorce? I could not possibly move out of this house. I can not support myself and the children on my own. I can not earn enough money. I do not want to work fulltime. My relationship with the children will be damaged. I can not stop crying. What should I do?

Now, the whole prospect of separation and divorce makes you feel ...

STAGE 4 – ANGER

I am angry with my spouse. I am mad at myself. I hate the paramour. I'm angry that this is happening to my life. All of my dreams are in ruins. I want my spouse to hurt as much as I am hurting. I want to make him or her pay. I'm going to make his or her "new life" miserable. I'm going to call up his or her paramour's spouse. I'm also going to tell his or her paramour what my spouse is really like. And his or her coworkers. And his or her family. And all of the friends we shared. Everyone needs to know that this is all his or her fault, that I am a victim, and just how much I and the children are suffering, all because of my spouse.

He or she is wrong and I am right. He or she is trying to control me, and I will not be controlled. I am going to get what I am entitled to. I want my day in court, to let everyone know I have been wronged. My spouse needs to be punished. I will get even, plus one.

After awhile a calmness should begin to settle in. If this does not occur naturally, professional help, and possibly short-term medication for situational depression may be necessary, to get to ...

STAGE 5 – ACCEPTANCE

This marriage is over. I have been holding on to an image of what my spouse used to be, could have been, or should be, but not what he or she is in reality. On a day-to-day basis my spouse creates more pain in my life than joy, and truly does not care how much I am hurting. I have to accept that life doesn't always turn out as planned, and is not always fair. Bad things can happen. I can not live this way anymore. I have to take care of myself. I have to be strong for the children, and I have to take care of them. My spouse saw a lawyer, is actually going to stand up to me for the first time, and isn't backing down. My spouse is no longer paying bills, and I need to do something now.

You have now come full circle – right back to "**What should I do, where do I start?**"

So ... now what?

Get informed.

Make a plan.

Get your thoughts sorted out.

Implement your plan.

Get your life back.

How?

Get Informed

Once you know that you have to "do something," the first step is to get informed as to your and your spouse's rights and obligations. Some information may be found on the internet, such as on www.divorcenet. com, but the internet may not be specific as to state laws on divorce, the most recent changes in state divorce laws, differences between rules, procedures and support guidelines in different counties, how the local judges view the law and the process, and how local judges have ruled in recent cases similar to yours.

You need to see a lawyer. Your sibling who went through a divorce, your uncle who is a non-family law attorney in another state, your family member who once worked or works in a law office, your hairdresser, your mechanic, your friends at the club and your colleagues, are not the best sources for legal information. And mother and father do not always know best, no matter how well-intentioned their concern.

The settlement you will sign off on, or the court order you will obtain through litigation, will probably be the most important legal document to affect your life. You will be making on your own, or will be receiving from a judge, decisions as to your children, your retirement, your house, child support, alimony and debt. What contract will you ever sign that could address more important issues than those! Make sure you do it right, whether through litigation or settlement, or through alternative dispute resolution such as mediation or collaboration.

Make a Plan

Once you are informed as to your options, and as to whether or not your goals are *realistic*, it is time to Make a Plan. Your own plan. Do not just react to how your spouse treats you on a day-to-day basis, or let him or her dictate the shape of your new life. Emotional roller coasters are no fun to ride.

Some of the possible courses of action that you might take are set forth below, in order from the most <u>drastic options, which **will** create deep and lasting animosity</u>, to the more desirable options. Extreme options are appropriate only in extreme situations, and should only be planned out with advice of counsel.

Perhaps you like a lot of drama, and want to shake the soda bottle before twisting off the cap. If you feel like giving a huge amount of your hard-earned money to lawyers, and if you feel like creating possible difficulties for yourself in court down the line, you may want to implement, or you may actually need to implement, some of the high conflict nuclear plans described below.

If your spouse is spending thousands of dollars each month on drugs, or is molesting your children, throw your spouse's stuff out on the street one day before trash day, and let him or her know that he or she better pick it all up real soon, change the locks on the former marital home which is in your sole name, and hand your spouse a no-trespass letter. Or withdraw all the funds from the joint accounts, back a moving truck up to the home when your spouse is away, clean everything out including the contents of the refrigerator, cancel all the utilities in your name, and drive out of state back home to your parents with the children.

Put your children into a new daycare, and do not authorize your spouse to pick them up. Get a post office box, so your spouse can't read your mail. Copy all the asset statements that are at home, or remove them and keep them elsewhere. Move the china and silver out of the house to another location. Ask the court to require your spouse to submit to a mental health or substance abuse evaluation, as a condition to any contact your spouse has with the children. Arrange to have your spouse arrested leaving the liquor store parking lot, for driving while intoxicated. Maybe transfer all of the joint assets into your own name, to pay off marital debt, and to fund contested and costly litigation.

If your spouse is violent, maybe you really do need to get a restraining order, due to significant immediate past physical abuse, and your reasonable apprehension of imminent bodily harm. File and follow through with that criminal complaint for family assault. Have your spouse charged with telephone harassment, or charged under the curse and abuse laws.

Maybe ask the Family Court to grant you exclusive possession of the jointly titled marital home and motor vehicle, along with temporary spousal support, child support and custody. Ask the court to order your spouse to refrain from terminating, or to restore, any necessary utility services, or ask the court to make your spouse pay for suitable alternative housing, and to pay the deposits to connect the utilities to that housing.

You may file an application for services with the child support enforcement agency, to seek an administrative support order and a payroll withholding order. Have your spouse's tax refund intercepted to pay any arrearages, or have a driver's or professional license suspended until all arrears are paid up, with interest.

You may need to file a fault divorce case if you have grounds, and file a motion to restrain your spouse's dissipation of marital assets. Install a keystroke logger on your computer, or take the family computer to a specialist to image the hard drive, so later on you can ask the court to allow you to analyze your spouse's use of that computer. Conduct a forensic analysis of your spouse's handheld and mobile cell phone devices. Find out if you can record telephone calls, and whether or not if you do, the recordings would be admissible at trial. Find out if you can put a GPS tracking device on your spouse's car, or a camera in the house. Find out whether all that effort is even a good idea. Or a really, really bad one.

You may need to have a hearing on temporary spousal support, custody, visitation or child support. Maybe ask the court for exclusive possession of the marital home, and money from your spouse for attorney's fees. If you have no money, but need to fight it out in court, you may find an attorney willing to place a voluntary lien for attorney's fees on the marital home, if allowed by state law, so you actually <u>can</u> afford to take your spouse on.

Perhaps the way to go is to tell your spouse in a safe location, such as at a counseling session, that the marriage is over, and that you want to discuss how to move on with your lives separately and amicably.

You may want to start changing your life insurance beneficiary designations, and your "pay on death" directions with banks and with financial institutions. Finally get that Will drawn up so your spouse doesn't receive all of your assets if you die. Or get a new Will drawn up to revoke the old one which leaves everything to your spouse. Remove your spouse as an authorized user on your credit cards. Start separating joint accounts.

Perhaps you will hire an attorney to draw up a proposed Property Settlement Agreement on your own individual behalf, for you and your spouse to negotiate in an adversarial manner, either with or without aggressive threats of what you will each do to each other if you go to court.

If you and your spouse can work together, another option would be to discuss the possibility of doing a collaborative divorce. If you handle your divorce collaboratively, each of you, with your own attorneys, can protect your individual interests, and can resolve all of the issues regarding the dissolution of your marriage without either one of you making threats, or trying to grab more of the marbles.

Or you and your spouse may decide to go to a court-certified attorney mediator specializing and litigating in local family law matters, to help educate you as to the family laws and local court system, to help you resolve your disagreements, and to draw up a binding and enforceable Agreement which will become a part of your final divorce order.

No matter which plan you think may be best, be sure to get input from at least one attorney, before you start skipping down a road which may lead you right off of a cliff. The direction in which you initially head will play a huge part in where you will eventually wind up.

Find an attorney with whom you are comfortable, and work with that attorney to determine the most advisable course of action for you. Good attorneys have concern for you, and want to help you and your family. Utilize the experience, knowledge and counsel which caring lawyers can provide.

Get Your Thoughts Sorted Out

To help deal with such a major life change as a divorce, it is a good idea to get into, or to stay in therapy, if you are struggling to control and sort out overwhelming emotions. There is no longer such stigma associated with taking care of your mental health needs. Judges like to see that people going through divorces are taking care of themselves. A divorce is supposed to be a traumatic event. It would be considered more unusual if you did not miss a beat going through such a disruptive occurrence in your life.

If necessary, get on prescribed medications to get your feelings under control, so that you are emotionally strong enough to make decisions, to work with your attorney and to be a parent to your children. Recognize that everything you are going through your children are also going through, even more so, and will need special attention and quite possibly some counseling themselves. Children are not equipped with the same tools as are adults to handle such emotional upheaval.

If you are married to an alcoholic, or are the child of an alcoholic, start reading about enablers, and about adult children of alcoholics. You are going to recognize yourself in the pages of these books, and will start to recognize your children. Break the cycle.

If you are in a relationship that brings you more pain than joy, start reading about codependency. Love is not real love if it is given "only if . . ." Real love is given *even so* and *no matter what*. If it's not real, leave before you have shut down so much of yourself that you no longer have any ability to feel.

If your spouse is abusing you and you have children, explore the very real options for help that shelters and other groups can provide, so that you will stop teaching your children that abuse is acceptable. If you will not get out of a physically abusive relationship, thinking that you are staying together "for the good of the children," stop deluding yourself. You are teaching your children all the wrong things, and they will most likely follow in both of their parents' footsteps.

If you are being verbally and physically abused by your spouse, once he gets older, your son will quite possibly also start verbally and physically abusing you, since as a little boy he was unable to protect you from your spouse. He may also abuse the women with whom he will have relationships in the future. And when your daughter who was not able to resolve your conflict gets older, she may seek out relationships with the same conflict, in subconscious hopes of fixing the unresolved problem.

Maybe you feel you have justifications for tolerating your spouse's abuse. Well then perhaps you should picture, and remember, the most humiliated and hurt your spouse has ever made you feel. Are you crying yet? Now picture your daughter going through that. Do you really want to keep giving her the message that this sort of thing should be tolerated in a marriage? Are you teaching the lesson that abuse should be accepted and hidden, to maintain a façade that your family is respectable and of good standing? Will your legacy to your children be to teach them that the one with the money and power can act badly, and that the weaker person should accept abuse for money, or to maintain an image or a lifestyle?

If you don't want the divorce, you will go from emotional highs if your spouse is nice to you, thinking "maybe we won't get divorced after all," to emotional lows when your spouse backs away. You'll drive yourself crazy going up and down emotionally. If your spouse wants the divorce and you don't, once your spouse sees you move from denial to acceptance, you are actually giving your spouse permission to be nice to you, because now your spouse knows that if he or she hugs you or shows you some tenderness, you won't be getting your hopes up anymore for a reconciliation. After all, your spouse on some level may actually still care about you, and may not really enjoy hurting you. Letting go removes your spouse's power over you.

If your spouse is committing adultery and you are still in denial, it is still important to make a plan. Your spouse may very well be getting ready to walk away from the marriage. Don't be caught unprepared.

Don't think, however, that going to court will solve all of your prob-lems. Some adulterous spouses will transfer their anger at themselves for the mess they're making to the "innocent" spouse, to spare them-selves from feeling any guilt. An angry adulterous spouse will come up with many reasons as to why the innocent spouse *drove* him or her to a new relationship, due to the "innocent" spouse's coldness, nagging, end-less criticism, bossiness, lack of warmth and unwillingness or inability to fulfill the adulterous spouse's physical and emotional needs.

There is usually some truth to each viewpoint regarding the circumstances and factors that led to the dissolution of your marriage. And of course the lawyers can and will embellish upon and will bring out all the "justifications" on each side for the deterioration of your marriage, as they conduct an analysis of your and your spouse's respective degrees of fault. You can then listen in court to your spouse describe all of your faults and inadequacies to the judge in detail, and listen as he or she tells the judge all about how much more attentive than you his or her new love is. Do you really want to go there?

On the other hand, some adulterous spouses feel really really guilty for the damage they're causing, especially when they have children. The spouse feeling really guilty often wants to sign something and be done quickly, almost as if signing off on an Agreement grants permission to leave the marriage, and to be free. Often the spouse feeling guilty will make overly generous offers. The more time goes by, however, and once such a spouse moves out and actually starts incurring more expenses and bills to pay, that generosity can begin to evaporate very rapidly. The best settlement for the innocent spouse often comes right when that innocent spouse is saying, "But I don't want a divorce. If I give my spouse a proposed Agreement, he or she will think that I do want a divorce, and I don't."

Your divorce lawyer may tell you, however, that spouses who cheat once usually continue to cheat, and that your marriage is probably over. A mental health provider specializing in post-affair marriage recovery may tell you otherwise. If you choose to listen to the lawyer, you may hear that this affair may be a symptom of a marriage that had already failed, and that the affair may very well not even be the first affair – just the first one you found out about - and will probably not be the last one either. The inability of your spouse to be faithful and intimate with you alone may indicate deeper problems. But even if the adulterous spouse never cheats again, you may never really get over the affair, especially if the extramarital relationship was emotional in nature, and not only physical. It will take a whole lot of work to recover the marriage, and you and your spouse may not be up to it.

The question may more realistically be <u>when</u> will you wind up getting divorced, not <u>if</u>, and what sort of financial and emotional damage will occur in the meantime, could be avoided, or could be postponed, until then. If you do reconcile, there are ways to formally nullify a written Agreement with a written Modification Agreement, but don't count on that happening. Get your best deal when it is offered, because that will almost certainly be the <u>final</u> deal as to property and support, which deal will be carved in stone.

If your spouse is telling you things like "I just need some space, no it's not you, no there's no one else, I just need space," chances are there quite possibly <u>is</u> someone else. Either an extramarital relationship has already started, or your spouse wants it to start, or it's a fantasy relationship in your spouse's head. Either way, the relationship is not with living breathing you, but is perhaps with someone else, real or imagined. Your spouse may just be breaking it to you slowly.

Set short term goals. Today I'll find a lawyer. Tomorrow I'll make the appointment. I'll see the lawyer next week. I'll decide what course of action to take by the end of the month. I'll start looking at housing options, educational opportunities and other job possibilities after the next holiday.

Don't think about the whole overwhelming, desired final result. Take one day and one small step at a time, but keep planning and taking those steps.

Implement Your Plan

Once you have become informed, made a plan and sorted out the mental and emotional turmoil in your mind, you need to get started. Work with the professionals you have selected to implement that plan. Stick to it. Don't waver. Reach out for support to stay strong, so you don't get discouraged and give up. Form an image in your mind of what is important to you, and focus on that image, until you achieve your goal. You can't get there unless you know where you're going.

As you begin your separation, you will have to face and accept the fact that one of the very hardest aspects of separating from your spouse, whether the separation is amicable or ugly, is the financial aspect. The reality is that one or two incomes in one household simply go further than those same one or two incomes in two households. You will have to increase your earnings, and tighten your belt. A lot of the "extras" will no longer be affordable. You may go into debt, or be forced into bankruptcy. You may have to borrow money, or may have to take out a loan from your retirement account. You will spend a lot of money on attorney's fees.

It will probably take about two years to get totally back on track, but you will get there. Those two years will go by faster than you think. There will be an end to the process, after which you will have turned your life around, and will no longer need to think about, or feel as if, you are still "going through the divorce."

Get Your Life Back

Walk this difficult road with dignity, holding your head high. You can't see where you're going if you're staring at your feet. Accept graciously the support of those who are willing to respectfully and knowledgeably help you through this. Look forward, not backward. Concentrate on the immediate. Prioritize. Take one step at a time, with the final goal clearly in mind. If you don't determine to succeed, you are destined to fail. Learn to accept that there is some uncertainty to the future, as you work to create it. You are on the verge of rediscovering who you are. Take the opportunity to renew your beliefs. Smile. Outclass your spouse. Don't stoop to a low level. Decide what is important, and what is not. Develop new interests. These are very real truths, and not mere platitudes.

Separation and divorce is a process, which has to go through all of its stages, at a certain pace, for each of you. Don't let yourself get stuck in grief, or in anger. You could let yourself stay there for years, while your spouse simply learns to tune you out, move on and be happy again.

Divorce, as any trial in life, is an opportunity for personal growth. You are being provided a motivation to develop the strength, character and integrity to better yourself, to turn your life around, and to inspire others such as your children. Your successes will carry over into every other aspect of your personal and professional life. It is not that parts of you are being torn away or destroyed, but rather the divorce experience, and the self-knowledge you gain, will help to define and develop the whole person you are becoming.

As you overcome each obstacle, your self esteem will increase. Just look at what you've been dealing with. You are stronger than you think. You can and will get through this. You can do it. If there's no one around to tell you this on a daily basis, take a moment each day to tell this to yourself.

However, know that even though your marriage is ending, that fact does not change the fact that you and your spouse genuinely enjoyed good times in the past. Your former life together was not all a lie, and is not erased by the ending of your marriage. You have every right to hold on to your happy memories of former days. They *were* good, and nothing can take that away.

If life is an ocean, divorce is a riptide. Don't let the ending of your marriage pull you down to dark places where you'll founder. Keep your chin up, and ride it out until you recover, overcome, take new bearings and safely reach shores of new possibilities.

You will find that you will rediscover who you are, you will get your life back and you will be happy once again. The process can be very liberating.

Get going.

Chapter Two

LITIGATION, NEGOTIATION, COLLABORATION AND MEDIATION - SHOULD I WORK IT OUT, OR FIGHT IT OUT?

ALL ABOUT LITIGATION

Two rational, intelligent, emotionally healthy people getting a divorce wouldn't want to let the court make all of the important decisions about their new, separated lives. Litigation is expensive. Attorney's fees can be around $400.00 or more per hour, and billable in 15 minute increments. That means that for your attorney to read a one page correspondence from the other attorney, and to mail a copy to you, you are paying that attorney $100.00, plus postage and copy paper. That is actual money no longer in your pocket. A contested, fully litigated divorce case can easily cost you $50,000.00, or double that. Each. Why would you spend your children's college money, your retirement or your home equity, to fight with your spouse in court? Wouldn't you rather take a nice, long cruise, first class?

And in court, the judge will probably hear only one or two days of testimony, starting at 10:00 a.m. and ending at 5:00 p.m., with an hour break for lunch. After taking into account each attorney's opening and closing statements, each side only has two or three hours to present all of his or her evidence. Two or three hours for one party to testify, for all of his or her witnesses to testify, and for any cross-examination of each witness. Based on this "snapshot" of the entire marriage, the judge will then make decisions which will profoundly affect each of you, and your children, for the rest of everyone's lives. Then the judge and the lawyers all go home leaving you with the result they created.

Litigation is always a gamble. The only certainty is that your lawyers will hit the jackpot if your case is really expensive.

Litigation is an old-fashioned way to resolve disputes. Litigation is a show which you and your cast of witnesses put on for a judge, directed and produced by your attorney. Sometimes the attorney thinks that he or she is also the star.

Litigation is a battle. Litigation is combat. Litigation is a fight to be won or lost. In reality, though, only the lawyers are guaranteed a win, because even if you emerge victorious, the "victory" costs a bundle to achieve. You and your spouse both lose. And if you have children, a contentious, litigated divorce case will cause deep, painful and lasting damage to everyone, including to yourself.

If you are contemplating custody litigation, put this image in your mind: You and your spouse are engaged in a tug of war between your two new homes. The dividing line between your school districts, or perhaps even the state line, is on the ground between you. The middle of the rope is tied around your child, and you are each trying to pull him or her towards your respective homes. Now imagine that the rope is around your child's neck as you each pull. Get the picture? That's custody litigation.

People usually choose to go to court for any one or more of the following reasons:

People litigate out of anger. One or the other person never got out of the anger stage of the breakup of the marriage, and insists on continuing the fight. The truth is, however, that eventually the person against whom all the anger is directed usually learns to cope with, and tune out, the angry person's anger, and simply gets on with his or her life. But the angry person stays angry, and that anger eats away more and more at him or her, often turning into illness, disease and dysfunction in future relationships. The nonangry person "wins" by being happy despite all the games the angry person plays, and despite all the turmoil the angry person tries to create.

People litigate out of fear. Sometimes a person fears that he or she can't get by on the offered financial arrangement. He or she thinks the court will come up with a better result. If you combine a fearful client with a lawyer motivated less by compassion, and more by the opportunity for personal financial gain, the attorney could play on those fears and drive up the cost of litigation. Yes, there are some attorneys out there who will do just that. The result is a case that won't settle for any reasonable resolution.

People litigate out of greed. Sometimes greed is related to fear, and sometimes it's just pure selfishness. "I want ... I deserve ... I'm not giving ... I'm entitled to ... I can't afford ... I earned it or worked for it, so I'm keeping it."

If one side will not reasonably settle a case, and the battle would cost less than the likely and reasonable potential gain, from a strictly financial analysis, litigation may be necessary. But if you factor in the time spent or missed from work, the emotional cost and the length of time the case will take, the battle may actually not be worth the stress. Sometimes the smarter choice is to just walk away. Don't kid yourself that "it's a matter of principle." "Principle" is just a matter of outlook, and your view may be distorted by emotion or by ego. Your outlook at the moment is just one of many valid ways in which the situation could be viewed. Your view may be wrong.

People litigate to play the victim. The human mind is powerful. We can convince ourselves of anything. We can use our minds to create a healthy, optimistic and caring view of the world if we choose, no matter the circumstances in which we find ourselves. Some people going through a divorce choose instead to delude themselves into a belief that they are a victim, and are therefore entitled to significant compensation from their spouse to punish that spouse, or to help ease the pain of their perceived wounds. And no matter what effort the other spouse puts forth to try to resolve the marital dissolution amicably, often the person holding onto a belief of victimhood will choose to not budge from that belief, instead of assuming some responsibility for the situation which has been created. It's easier to blame others, and to maybe rewrite history in the process.

People litigate for control. Some people simply have to call all the shots. They will not work anything out. They may have mental health or substance abuse issues. They think they are smarter and better than their spouse and everyone else on the planet. They may appear quite charming to the outside world, but they insist on always getting their way. They may be absolute liars and actually believe their stories. What they want may be totally unreasonable. Angry, controlling, demanding, greedy people with mental health issues, substance abuse issues or inflated ego issues, who have unreasonable expectations of what they could get in court, are not the best candidates to amicably resolve the dissolution of their marriages.

People litigate for leverage. Your spouse may need to learn that this time you are serious. If you are on the lower end of a situation where there is unequal out-of-court bargaining power, commencing litigation may serve to strengthen your negotiating position. Your case may even settle well before you and your spouse deplete the family fortune. Perhaps you will employ a neutral third party to evaluate your court case, and to help you and your spouse, each with your respective attorneys, settle the pending litigation. Some groups employing retired judges offer such services, as do the Neutral Case Evaluation and

Settlement Conference Programs of some courts. However, if your court case will not settle, completing the litigation may then be the only way to obtain your best possible result.

Here are some truths about litigation:

Lawyers can argue both sides of anything.

You may have a "strong" case. That means your lawyer has some good arguments as to why the judge should "rule your way" based on the existing statutory and case law. Meanwhile, your spouse's lawyer is saying the very same thing to your spouse, because that lawyer can also think up some really good arguments, and can also find some statutory or case law somewhere to support those arguments.

Law is not an exact science. When you go to court, there are several questions which can be asked, and the important questions can be asked in many different ways. You and your spouse will advocate different answers to those different questions. In the end, you may find that the judge's ruling answers questions neither of you had even asked, with answers neither of you had suggested.

Lawyers are friends, or at least have professional collegial relations.

The "my lawyer can beat up your lawyer" mentality caters to a mistaken belief that your lawyer is some sort of weapon you can unleash for your personal use. Your very own gladiator. The reality is that most family law attorneys go to the same bar association functions, go to the same continuing legal education classes, have many cases with each other over the years and may even be friends. However, we will still fight the fight and try to win. We may even get ugly with each other, and file cross motions for sanctions, but it's not our battle – it's yours. It's competition to us to see who prevails, but it's your life. When it's all over, we lawyers will take the gloves off, go get some coffee together, congratulate the good work the other did, and refer future cases to each other. We do care about you, your life and your children, and truly do want to help you, but when your case is over, we lawyers go back to our offices and begin to prepare the next case. And your Invoice for Professional Services Rendered.

Judges do what they want.

Sure, we lawyers tell you all about the family laws. You'll learn of the statutory factors, and of the relevant cases the court will consider. You'll hear all about separate property, marital property and hybrid property, or about community property. You'll learn about "imputed income." But you'll also hear that we may have no clear idea as to how the judge in your case will rule on certain aspects regarding the division of your property, and that we may have no clear idea as to how the judge will rule on spousal support, because not all judges rule the same way on the same facts. Ten experienced, conscientious judges, listening carefully to all of the facts of your case, could come up with ten different solutions to your family situation. In the end, the judge will call upon his or her personal beliefs, along with impressions of you, your spouse and of the evidence, and will then do whatever he or she feels is just, based upon the principles which he or she will apply.

You may not agree with the judge. Your lawyer may even tell you that the Court of Appeals wouldn't agree with the judge, but the truth is most divorce cases are not appealed. Appeals cost a lot of money, and of those cases that are appealed, the standard on review is usually an inquiry into whether or not the judge "abused his or her discretion." So even if the judge (in your opinion) ruled erroneously, you'd pretty much have to prove that the judge did so without considering the evidence. Most judges will be sure the record shows they "considered" all the relevant evidence, and that evidence will be considered by the Court of Appeals in the light most favorable to the party who prevailed in the trial court. It's tough to win on appeal, especially if you are trying to reverse a well- respected judge, who has properly recited into the record detailed reasons for his or her conclusions.

No one wins it all.

In a fully litigated divorce case, there may be ten or twenty or more things for the judge to rule on. The house. The value of the house. The pension or pensions. Separate premarital or post-separation portions of assets. Increases in equity attributable to those separate portions. Post-separation reduction in principle attributable to post-separation mortgage payments. IRAs. Alternate valuation dates. Alimony – permanent, rehabilitative or none. Imputed income. Custody - sole, joint legal, split or shared. Primary residence. Visitation – ninety days or less, ninety days or more; why is that important? Particulars of visitation. Child support. Health insurance. Medical expenses not covered or reimbursed by insurance. Tax exemptions. Tax refunds or further liability. Life Insurance. Debt. All of those items set forth in Appendix 4 of this *Guide,* entitled *General List of Topics to be Resolved.*

Picture a balloon. You squeeze one part here, and it comes out somewhere else over there. You may "win" on spousal support, and then get hit on attorney's fees. The judge may choose your spouse's value for the business interest, and not your value. You may get your separate premarital down payment on the former marital home back, but the judge decides not to also award you the increase in equity attributable to that separate interest, because the resulting division of equity would be grossly unfair.

If you think divorce is a contest to be won in a courtroom, understand that only the lawyers paid to fight the fight really win. Even if the judge grants you your main requests, after the time you have spent, the attorney's fees, the emotional costs and the effects on your family are considered, you have lost a lot. You may have irreparably scorched the earth you and your children are standing on.

You won't get everything. You'll spend a fortune. You won't be entirely happy with the result, and neither will your spouse. It'll all be over faster than you'd have thought, and you're left with the result. Your lawyer will send you a big bill for all the legal work done, and will move on to his or her next big case. Was it worth it?

Sometimes it is, usually it is not. What are the alternatives?

ALL ABOUT NEGOTIATION

Even though you may know what a court would likely award your spouse, you *do* have the right to make him or her work for it. You don't have to just hand it to him or her on a silver platter, with gravy and a decorative little garnish.

If you are going through a divorce, you will want to feel that you have a lawyer protecting your individual interests. Most lawyers will begin an adversarial process, will threaten or commence litigation, will make a variety of blustery arguments to the other side, and will eventually settle your case. Yes, most cases do eventually settle. The vast, overwhelming majority are resolved through compromise.

Settlement is an art. Lawyers practice this art all day long, every day. We don't mind conflict. For us family law attorneys, our professional lives deal with nothing but conflict. We're comfortable with all forms of conflict. We're good at it, although some are better than others. We don't get nervous if the police are called. We can be reasonable, unreasonable, tough, approachable, compassionate or all of those in any one day, or hour, depending upon the cases we're working on. We may settle early on in the case, or on the day of trial.

It is important to have a lawyer who has put your case in the best possible posture for litigation, in order to get the best possible settlement. There is a great variety of attorneys from which to choose, and your choice will greatly affect the strength of your case, and the point at which your case will settle. For more on this important topic, please see Chapter 3 of this *Guide,* entitled *How Do I Choose a Divorce Lawyer for Litigation or for Negotiation?*

However, the point at which a case settles depends largely upon you and your spouse. You are the ones who are trying to find that agreed upon custody arrangement, or happy dollar amount. Regarding financial issues, look at it this way: there is some number which is the most one of you will pay, and there is some number which is the least the other of you will accept. Good lawyers will find that number, and will help you to settle your case for that amount. Better lawyers will move the point of settlement more one way or the other. Even better lawyers will jointly push you together if your points don't quite touch, because the difference between your two numbers is probably less than the cost to go to court. There are a few "bad" lawyers out there who will keep you apart so you will not settle, and so they will get to charge you for a contested case.

Is negotiation with two lawyers the way to go? Let's see. You tell your attorney what you want. Your attorney writes something up for you to review, then confirms that it is exactly what you want. Then your attorney sends your proposal to the other attorney. The other attorney tells your spouse what you want. Your spouse tells his or her attorney what he or she thinks of your proposal, and that attorney and your spouse verify that your spouse's attorney understands your spouse's response. Your spouse's attorney then tells your attorney what your spouse thinks of what you want. Your attorney finally tells you what your spouse thinks about what you want. You do this thumbs up/ thumbs down over and over again, addressing item after item, perhaps one item at a time, slowly moving closer to a resolution.

For some the back and forth exchange described above may be the best way to safely resolve those matters which can be settled relatively easily, while advocating your interests in the tougher areas. However, you will almost certainly each be billed the time for every telephone call, letter, email and document preparation, plus for postage, photocopies and fax paper, as your attorney acts as your mouthpiece. Wouldn't it be less costly for all four of you to communicate within one room? Or maybe, better yet, for you and your spouse to actually communicate directly with each other?

Sometimes, however, you and your spouse can not communicate with each other. There's still a bit too much anger. If you are intimidated by your spouse, the playing field may not be level. Maybe you never did learn how to communicate, and that's why you're getting divorced in the first place. You may therefore have no choice but to litigate, or to negotiate.

Before entering into involved settlement discussions, and before running off to court, it is essential that you first become informed as to the law, as to the divorce process and as to what is reasonable to expect. You may find that creative solutions are generated through nonadversarial negotiation in attorney-to-attorney exchanges, or in four-way conferences. You may even possibly find that if you participate in the litigation process, the litigation might proceed smoothly, professionally and without animosity.

ALL ABOUT MEDIATION

Not everyone getting a divorce feels that they have to hate each other. You don't have to become enemies just because you can't live with each other anymore. You may want to remain friends when it's all over.

If you and your spouse can communicate with each other, and if you both want to take part in creating your future, together you can decide how to settle everything. You can even be creative, and can make limited preliminary agreements to release money in part, or to just sell the house. You can make partial agreements. You can experiment with custody arrangements, through short term or temporary agreements, to find out what works best.

Litigation is a poor and rather outdated way to resolve family disputes. Litigation will usually hurt you in some way. Hiring attorneys to fight your fight in court is expensive, antagonistic and causes lasting animosity. You and your spouse lose all control over your lives, and the money you are fighting over goes to your attorneys instead of to you. The result will be dictated to you by a judge, who is a stranger to your family.

If you choose instead to work out your case through alternative dispute resolution, you can achieve results tailored to your special needs, you will probably both be happier, and you and your spouse will be much more likely to resolve future problems amicably. You may each even choose to be generous. You might still even like and respect each other when it's all over.

If you and your spouse can communicate with each other, and would rather your money go to your own family and not to your lawyers' families, you may want to consider mediation. If you can work it out, it will work for both of you.

You may each hire separate lawyers, just to provide individual legal advice and information to you. That advice and information will form a basis for the decision-making in mediation. You may then ask your separate attorneys to review, and to comment upon, a proposed draft Mediated Agreement prepared by the mediator, which Agreement you feel ready to sign, to ensure that the Agreement is in your best interests, and that it covers all of your interests.

If you mediate your divorce, you and your spouse will sit at a table with, or in the office of, an experienced, neutral third party. This mediator will help you to resolve your differences.

First, you will have an initial discussion to make sure you and your spouse understand the style of the mediator, and what he or she, or occasionally a pair of comediators, can do for you. Is the mediator's style purely facilitative, helping you to determine only what you voice as important to you, without mentioning those matters you haven't thought of, or of which you are not aware? Evaluative, letting you know what the mediator believes a judge would be likely to do? Directive, trying to influence or advise one or both of you, perhaps improperly? Transformative, trying to help you to see things in a new light? Faith-based, where Christian biblical or other religious principles may be considered and referred to in the resolution of your differences?

Or Informative, where the mediator will give you a lot of information about the law, about what topics you need to address, and about what options you have? Where you will both be provided, right in front of the other, with the legal information attorneys separately representing each of you would likely provide? Who will then write up a binding and enforceable settlement of your divorce?

At the commencement of the process, you and your spouse will each describe the situation to be mediated from your individual perspectives. You will then each identify your respective concerns, and will summarize and order those concerns. To gather some momentum, you may then identify common ground, or you may start right with the problematic areas, and the rest will fall into place.

You may need to obtain further information regarding the values and division of some of your assets, such as your house, the retirement plans or maybe a business. You and your spouse may decide to meet, either together or separately, with a trust and estate attorney, tax accountant, financial planner, retirement benefits specialist, mortgage lender and/or family therapist, to discuss and generate options, or to obtain individual advice. Or you may choose instead to involve any of these specialists in the actual mediation sessions.

Understand that you must voluntarily share information, including statements pertaining to all of your assets and pertaining to all of your debt, since mediation requires full disclosure. If you do not fully disclose all relevant information during the process, the Agreement you sign off on in the end could be voided by law.

After all information is disclosed and analyzed, you will then each propose possible solutions in the areas where you are not in agreement, and will evaluate those options. Your interests will be discussed. The mediator may have some ideas as to possible solutions you hadn't even thought of. Maybe you will think about how realistic some of the proposals are should the case go to court.

You will decide upon solutions where possible, and the decisions will be embodied in a document. You may then each go to your separate lawyers to see if you all missed something, or to make sure the document protects you. If it does, you sign and you're done. All that is left is for one of you to then go to a lawyer who did not mediate for you, and to file the actual divorce case in the court. Your Mediated Agreement will become a part of the final divorce order.

Mediation should be a confidential process, so that you and your spouse can explore the widest possible range of settlement options. You should feel free to take conciliatory positions in mediation which you would not take in court. You should not be made to fear that if the mediation fails, either of you could go to court and tell the judge what the other would have agreed to in mediation. The Agreement to Mediate you will sign should state that the mediator, and the mediator's notes, can not be subpoenaed for court.

Chances are excellent that if you and your spouse are both committed to working it out, you will. You will fashion your own solution, instead of leaving it to the courts. You will both take control out of the judge's hands, and will put your life's new direction in your own hands. You will not be stuck with a binding court order, without first having worked out what is best for you.

There is a great variety of mediators from which to choose, and your choice will greatly affect how your mediation progresses. For more on this important topic, please see Chapter 5 of this *Guide,* entitled *How Do I Choose a Family Law Mediator?*

ALL ABOUT THE COLLABORATIVE PROCESS

You may feel, however, that you need someone "on your side" protecting your individual interests, and that the mediator is too neutral for your liking. If you are in an abusive relationship, mediation may be inappropriate. You may want a lawyer to help you, but you "don't want it to get adversarial." You may then want to explore the possibility of resolving your divorce collaboratively.

What is a collaborative divorce?

Collaboration is like mediation, in that you are working to privately settle your differences outside of court, except you each have your own lawyer protecting your individual rights and supporting you, and you won't even make threats about what you could do if you don't settle. All four of you are committed to working out your differences without fighting it out through litigation.

The collaborative process essentially involves a series of sit-downs with you and your spouse, along with each of your attorneys. You approach the dissolution of your marriage in a creative, problem-solving way, not in a combative way. No one is trying to grab all of the marbles; you are simply working it all out. If you can't work it out, you have to go get new lawyers to do the combative lawyer thing, but if you do work it out, your lawyers can complete the divorce in court.

The attorneys must be trained in collaborative practice. However, there are no set rules governing how collaborative cases must be handled, other than a requirement that you, your spouse and your attorneys all sign a four-way Collaborative Contract, whereby you all agree to do a collaborative divorce. **That contract must say that if the collaboration fails, you will each have to go get new lawyers.** Any other requirements as to how the process is best handled relate to the preferences, expertise and recommendations of the collaborative attorney.

The disqualification of the attorneys if the case doesn't get worked out, and winds up in court, is what makes the case a collaborative case. If your Collaborative Contract does not contain a provision stating that the attorneys can not represent you anymore if the collaboration fails, your case may be a negotiated case which may settle without going to court, or a "cooperative" case, but not a collaborative case. You may choose to use a team model involving neutral financial and mental health professionals, or you may choose not to. Either approach is valid, and either approach may be the right approach for you.

The Collaborative Contract will usually also state that during the process, you won't make threats about what you could do if you decide later on to go to court instead of settling. During the collaboration, your attorneys may each advocate for you, and may separately advise you, but will not be adversarial or combative. You are all there strictly to work things out. However, if you just can't work it all out, you can always terminate the collaborative process, and can then go to court with new attorneys.

If you and your spouse each know from the outset that you want to do a collaborative divorce together, you will each sign a Representation Agreement with your respective attorneys, hiring your attorneys for collaborative representation.

If you want to do a collaborative divorce, but are not sure your spouse is willing, you or your attorney could give your spouse information about the collaborative process. You may also provide your spouse with a list of collaborative attorneys in the area. Your attorney may recommend a few specific local collaborative attorneys with whom he or she is comfortable collaborating, because those attorneys will approach the process in the same way as your attorney. Generally attorneys in the same geographic area will collaborate in similar ways, and will know each other pretty well.

Once your spouse is on board, and has hired an attorney for collaborative representation, there will be an overview by each attorney with his or her client describing how that attorney conducts his or her collaborative practice. The two attorneys may have also collaborated together previously on other cases, and will set the parameters with each other as to how they will work together.

In separate meetings, each of you, with your attorneys, will go over your respective concerns, and will review the applicable law. In the Collaborative Process, just as in litigation, in negotiation or in mediation, it is still very important to know the applicable divorce laws of your state, and how they would be applied by your local courts. You will then each prepare for your first four-way meeting, and will each review the Collaborative Contract with your attorneys prior to the meeting at which the Contract will be signed.

Prior to the first meeting, the lawyers will also touch base with each other as to what will be addressed at that meeting, but they will not strategize as to the outcome. Perhaps there are some pressing issues which need to be addressed early on in the process to protect each of you, such as the filing of a support motion to preserve the retroactivity of support, or the submission of an agreed order restraining the dissipation of marital assets. Your rights should not be compromised in any way due to your participation in the collaborative process.

At the first meeting, the process and confidentiality issues will be discussed, and the Collaborative Contract will be signed. You will each present your concerns, emphasizing any immediate priorities such as custody or visitation, and will discuss and agree upon the participation of any third parties in the process. Information will then be gathered, and will be shared at subsequent meetings.

As with mediation, together you will generate, evaluate and agree upon workable options during the process. You and your spouse will each meet with your individual attorneys between meetings, and the lawyers will also touch base between meetings. They may even prepare Minutes of each meeting to clarify what was discussed, and may prepare Agendas after each meeting to clarify what will be addressed next. Eventually a Collaborative Settlement Agreement will be drafted by one of the attorneys, and will be signed by you and your spouse. The attorneys will then prepare the court papers to finalize the divorce, along with any necessary retirement court orders.

The collaborative attorneys handling your divorce may involve other professionals in the collaborative process, such as financial specialists and mental health specialists. Some collaborative attorneys will speak of "allied professionals," or "consultants," to describe the non-legal professionals or experts who may be a part of the process. You and your spouse may meet together with a financial specialist, or with a child specialist, outside of the four-way meetings, without your attorneys present. Or you may choose instead to involve the non-attorney professionals in the four-way meetings.

You may choose to each have a personal mental health coach available for you until the process is completed, to help you be strong, to help you participate effectively and to help you clearly convey your interests. You may choose to have one mental health professional work with both of you, to help create a deep and clear understanding of each of your thoughts. Coaches can assist you in moving forward constructively, so that you and your spouse will be better able to parent your children together in the future. Or you may choose to proceed without the participation of any mental health specialists at all.

Any neutral professionals you choose to involve in the process will each sign a Participation Agreement, which Agreement will address confidentiality issues, and will address the open sharing of information. Each Agreement will also state that the professional will be barred from testifying in court if the case does not settle. The ethical requirements binding the professional may also prohibit that professional from being able to help either of you in the future after you are divorced.

As with mediation, collaboration requires full disclosure. Some collaborative attorneys feel the process should be so transparent that the lawyers won't even advise their clients as to strategy, or as to the law, unless the other party and his or her attorney are also present. Other collaborative practitioners feel that an attorney can be an advocate for his or her client's interests without being adversarial, and will hold separate meetings with his or her client to strategize, and to address the client's concerns, throughout the process.

As with the use of the mediation process, if you and your spouse are serious about settling your case using the collaborative process, you will settle. Also, as with mediation, collaboration is respectful, private, more economical than litigation, more dignified than litigation, and will certainly preserve your family relationships while resolving your marital relationship. The process, however, is not inexpensive. The benefit is that you have the opportunity to gain deeper insight into some of the emotional, psychological and financial issues surrounding the breakup of the marriage than you would have gained using traditional negotiation. You can then use that insight to determine how best to move forward.

There is a great variety of collaborative lawyers from which to choose, and your choice will greatly affect the speed, the cost and the approach taken in your collaborative process. For more on this important topic, please see Chapter 6 of this *Guide,* entitled *How Do I Choose a Collaborative Divorce Attorney?*

SO SHOULD I WORK IT OUT THE EASY WAY, OR FIGHT IT OUT THE HARD WAY?

Your case may address the division of large business interests involving government contracts, protective orders and nondisclosure agreements. You may be dissolving a large asset marriage encompassing multiple properties, and numerous investments. Or you may have a "garden variety" divorce involving a house, some retirement, two or three cars, spousal support and some credit card debt. Perhaps you are mainly concerned with trying to find out what is best for your children.

In any of these cases, mediation or collaboration, possibly involving a mutually agreed upon financial analyst, retirement benefits specialist or child psychologist, can be the best way to go. The costs and animosity will be significantly lower than if you were to litigate. You will be fully informed.

Nonadversarial mediation or collaboration is more private than the spectacle of public litigation, and you and your spouse most definitely have a much better chance of getting along with each other when it is all over. You will have the opportunity to test ideas out during the process, which can help you to fine tune and tailor the solutions to your particular situation. You may even develop and learn better ways to communicate with each other, and to resolve future difficulties amicably.

However, you may have no choice but to fight. *You* may want to settle, but your spouse won't. Perhaps he or she is being aggressive, passive-aggressive or just downright unreasonable.

If you are dealing with an abusive or controlling spouse, if there are mental health or substance abuse problems, if your spouse is making grossly unfair or no offers of settlement, if your spouse's participation in mediation or in the collaborative process would only be in bad faith, or if you really want to "have your day in court" you may have to go down the tough path of adversarial litigation, or of aggressive negotiation.

Most important of all is that you shop around, talk to attorneys and to mediators, and choose the person with whom you feel most comfortable to guide you down whichever path you take. In a very real sense, you will be placing your future, and all that you hold dear, in that person's hands, as he or she helps you through what may be the most difficult time of your life. If you can not work with your attorney, your attorney can not work for you.

Live your life, and make decisions based on what is best for you and for your children, not necessarily based upon "how it will look in court." Granted, you do not want to jeopardize your case with damaging courses of action, but don't damage your life because you were worried about how a course of action might play out in court. Remember that if you wind up in court, lawyers can argue both sides of anything. We can also take the facts before us, find the good in a situation, and cast what we have in the best possible light.

No matter how tarnished you are, we'll manage to make you shine.

Chapter Three

HOW DO I CHOOSE A DIVORCE LAWYER FOR LITIGATION OR FOR NEGOTIATION?

Why do I even need a lawyer? Can't I just do it on my own?

Not a good idea.

Especially if the dissolution of your marriage involves spousal support, the division of retirement assets, or any asset into which premarital or "separate" money may have been invested. You need legal information, and you need an attorney to properly draft your documents. It's just too important not to do right. The IRS could come after you. The omission or inclusion of a simple word like "modifiable" or "reservation" or "waiver" in the same sentence as the words "spousal support" will have permanent implications for you.

You are not a lawyer. You may know some of the important points to resolve, but you don't know what you are not even aware of. It is your attorney's job to help you address points in the minefield of legal issues which you haven't even thought of, such as, is a capital loss tax carryover a marital asset? Frequent flyer miles? Unused earned leave? Does life insurance have a cash value? Who is entitled to the dependency exemptions for the children?

Drafting your own documents is analogous to having your mechanic do your root canal, or having your barber do your home's electrical wiring. If the job isn't done right, something really important could blow up.

What if it's only a "simple" divorce, with no children and no assets? Can't I handle that on my own?

You still should probably not do your divorce by yourself. Divorce is a creature of state law, and marriages must be resolved by a court case with a final court order. Think of it this way - can you sew? If you tear open your hand, you could probably take a needle and thread, and close the wound, but the process will be painful, and the result may not be right in the end. Sure, a surgeon can practically do the stitches in his or her sleep, and it's no big deal to him or her. That's why you pay for his or her education, training and experience. You do not have that education, training and experience.

If you do your own divorce, it may feel like you are studying for that big exam, and writing that term paper, every day for a year. The divorce court clerks can't help you with your filings, because they can not give you legal advice, and are unauthorized to practice law. The local bar association or divorce court clerk may have some forms, but if you don't know what you are doing with the language in those forms, trying to get your divorce on your own will be a long and difficult process. You will quite possibly then wind up with an erroneous if not disastrous result.

Okay, so if I need a lawyer, what do I look for, or look out for?

What sorts of lawyers are out there?

All kinds.

First of all, you want a family law specialist. The lawyer who helped you with your traffic ticket, or who prepared your Last Will and Testament, may know much less about the ins and outs of divorce than someone who practices family law exclusively. Would you go to your eye doctor for a heart problem, or to your dermatologist for a broken bone? The law is highly specialized. It is very hard for a general practitioner to have in-depth knowledge and great expertise in every area of the law.

Are the lawyers in the large firms the best?

There are good lawyers in big firms and bad ones, just as in medium size firms, in small firms and in solo practices. Most large firms are somewhat "tiered," with the senior partners charging very high fees, senior and junior associates charging less and the paralegal who does much of the paperwork charging at an even lower hourly fee. The big name lawyer "supervising the team" may actually have very little involvement with your case. You may find that there never seems to be just one individual who knows everything about your situation, and your billing invoices may show "meetings" between attorneys in the firm chatting with each other about your case, to bring each other up to speed.

And yes, you are paying for the marble hallway, original artwork in the reception area, and for the monogrammed napkins embossed with the firm logo. You are also helping to pay for your attorney's pricey suits, European vacations and luxury cars, but you get to tell all of your friends that your divorce is being "handled" by that prominent, well-known attorney. The one with the expensive cuff links or jewelry.

<u>What should I look for in choosing a lawyer?</u>

Experience and Ability. You want someone who knows what he or she is doing. If you are mainly concerned with resolving custody arrangements, ask your attorney just how many custody cases he or she has litigated and won. Would you feel comfortable hiring a surgeon for a delicate operation which he or she has never before performed? If you are concerned about your interest in a marital business, or in a professional practice, ask your attorney how many cases he or she has handled that involved business interests. You want someone who is good at what he or she is doing, who has done it before, and who knows how to get the job done.

Understanding and Compassion. You want your attorney to actually listen to you, to answer your questions, to understand what you wish to achieve and to actually care about helping you to achieve it. During the initial consultation, see if the attorney you are interviewing constantly interrupts and talks over you, or whether he or she lets you express your concerns when you converse. It may help you a great deal, and mean a lot to you, to have an attorney who will provide some encouragement and support to you, as opposed to hiring an attorney who doesn't listen to you, or who makes you feel as if he or she is only interested in timing his or her speeches to you, and then billing you for them.

Organization. You want an attorney who is accessible, who responds timely to your requests, who doesn't forget the particulars of your situation, who is organized with respect to managing his or her calendar so you are not kept waiting, and who is organized in terms of managing the documents which will seem to multiply on their own in your file. It's nice if your attorney can remember your child's name in court. And yours.

Able to Educate. If you are going to present your case in court, you will need to understand the applicable statutes, and you will need to understand the procedures applicable to your county courthouse. Your attorney should be able to communicate to you the points you will need to convey to the judge, and must be able to explain to you the manner in which you will express those points.

Not Overbooked. Some attorneys just can't say no to any fee that walks in the door, with the result that they frequently overextend themselves, and often do not prepare adequately for trial. You need for your attorney to pay attention to what is going on in your case, to keep you up to date, to timely return your telephone calls and emails, and to prepare you for your hearings. You don't want to be just another folder in the pile, especially if you stay on the bottom of that pile until the day before court.

What should I watch out for in choosing a lawyer?

Excessive fees spent pursuing unrealistic positions. Watch out for lawyers who pump you up with unreasonable expectations, so they can charge you for a big case. Danger signs include some of the following:

If your attorney tells you that the judge should and will give you at least $10,000 per month in spousal support, ask that attorney just how many times he or she has achieved that result in litigated court cases, with incomes and facts similar to yours, as opposed to settled cases. Ask the attorney in which counties he or she litigated those cases, and then go look them up under the lawyer's name. Divorce cases are a matter of public record, and you should try to verify your attorney's big claims.

If your attorney tells you that the judge will punish your spouse for his or her adultery or desertion by giving you 70% or more of the marital assets, ask that attorney how many times he or she has obtained that result in litigated cases in the local courts. Then go look those cases up. Did the facts of the adultery include long-term deception, a child born out of wedlock or a sexually transmitted disease? Find out exactly how your local judges usually rule on fault claims.

And even if you were to get 70% of the home equity, and 70% of the retirement, if you fully and publicly litigated your case, do a reality check. Exactly how many dollars more than if there were a 50/50 split would you ultimately end up with once you pay off your attorney? Your attorney may be more interested in his or her own compensation than in yours.

If your lawyer tells you that your spouse will have to pay all of your attorney's fees, ask that attorney exactly how much money in fees any judge has ever awarded in his or her litigated cases. Was it more than $20,000? More than 20 percent? Actually 50 percent? And what were the total fees in the case? $50,000? $80,000? $100,000? Ask the attorney in which counties he or she litigated those cases, and then try to look them up. If there were large attorneys fees awards, just how egregious were the facts in those cases? Will your case actually be as acrimonious?

Is your attorney telling you that the local judges in a contested custody case will give sole physical custody, or shared physical custody, to you, a good father, even if there is absolutely nothing wrong with the mother, such as significant untreated mental health issues, substance abuse problems or cohabitation? Ask for the counties for the cases where the attorney obtained that result through litigation, and then try to look them up.

Does it make any difference to the other lawyer, or to the judge, whether my attorney is male or female, or young or old?

No.

Does it matter whether or not I use a lawyer local to where the case will be litigated?

Absolutely.

Each county is different. Unless your attorney practices regularly in several counties, and is known by the judges in each of those counties, it is usually best to have a local attorney familiar with the local practices, familiar with the local judges, and with whom the local judges are familiar. It just is.

Do attorneys have different styles?

Yes.

Some attorneys have reputations for never settling. They will drag you painfully through every step of the process, at great cost to both you and to your spouse. They may be aggressive and flamboyant about it, or rather passive and low key. Both types are expensive.

On the other hand, some attorneys settle cases very quickly. Too quickly. Some lawyers who don't like going to court will give away too much.

Some attorneys have been lawyers for decades, and still do things the old tried and true way. They may be unwilling to communicate with you by email, and do not have voicemail. Others may routinely check their email and voicemail remotely from home at night and on weekends, and don't mind shooting you quick responses to short questions electronically.

Some attorneys, (a small minority), can be somewhat hostile, and will not work amicably towards any settlement. They will expend a lot of effort throwing gasoline onto the fire. The problem with that approach is that you, your spouse and your children are what gets burned.

If your attorney tells you not to talk to your spouse, that "everything should go through the lawyers," and that you should "leave it all up to the judge to decide," your attorney may be making your divorce more costly than it need be. You should talk to your spouse. Just don't sign anything without your attorney's input, and don't let your spouse bully you. The more you and your spouse can work out together, the less you will each have to pay your lawyers to work out. Beware of any attorney who tries to increase hostility, and who tries to keep you from talking settlement with your spouse.

Some attorneys have reputations for being very good or very competent, very reasonable and very open to settlement. They are compassionate, conscientious and know the law.

Some attorneys have reputations as aggressive and tough negotiators, who will only settle once they have fully prepared the case for litigation. Other attorneys may consider those attorneys to be unreasonable for not settling earlier, before so much money is spent on attorney's fees unnecessarily.

A few attorneys may be pretty bad. The scary thing is that you may never even realize that your case wasn't handled properly, unless you obtained a second opinion on your case. Yes, you have the right to do that at any time. You can even switch lawyers, unless it's too late.

Does having two lawyers involved to negotiate or litigate a case mean that it has to get ugly?

No.

The lawyers do not have a personal stake in your case, except perhaps a friendly competition to win on the bigger issues, for bragging rights with other lawyers about their general successes. Lawyers can conduct a fully litigated case in a professional, courteous, respectful and ethical manner, and do not have to be mean to be adversarial. If the two attorneys in a case start to feel personal animosity for each other, the case is probably in trouble.

You do not want your attorney's objectivity to be colored by some personal agenda unrelated to the merits of your case. Watch out for any attorney who seems to have a personal chip on his or her shoulder. And no, your spouse's attorney isn't motivated by a personal desire to harass you. He or she has nothing against you, and would have let you hire him or her yourself if you had tried to do so before your spouse did.

Will the lawyer be expensive?

Yes.

Ask right up front how much the divorce could cost if it were to be fully contested. Not all lawyers want to scare you away with the information that a fully litigated divorce case could be upwards of $30,000, $50,000, or $80,000. Each.

Watch out for lawyers who try to hook you in for a minimum down payment divorce, but who then bill hourly. Almost all attorneys bill divorce cases hourly. Once your case becomes contested, that minimum fee vanishes, and you start getting monthly bills for $3,000, $5,000, $8,000 … with no end in sight. Yes, *monthly*.

Will your attorney just stop working on your case if you don't keep up with the invoices? Or withdraw as your counsel, leaving you to represent yourself? He or she shouldn't do the former, and may do the later.

When you interview attorneys, ask each attorney how long he or she gives a client to pay the final bill. Has he or she sued former clients to collect fees? It could be unsettling for you to realize that all of that aggressiveness you wanted to unleash upon your spouse could be unleashed upon you, if your lawyer is not paid.

You want to hear that it will only be $2,000 to get divorced, and when you put your $2,000 down, you are hoping you won't have to make another payment for a long time, if at all. But to complete proceedings for temporary custody and support, you could easily spend $10,000 to $15,000 each. A properly litigated custody case alone, with witnesses, could easily cost $20,000 each. Know what you're getting into before you're too deeply into it.

So watch out for, and don't get hooked by statements like: "You deserve more than fifty percent of the assets because of what your spouse did to you. The judge will impute income to her, so you won't have to pay support. The judge will impute income to him, so he will have to pay you more support. Don't worry about the attorney's fees."

You should be worried. Be very worried.

Chapter Four

ADVERSARIAL SETTLEMENT

Even though you and your spouse are posturing your cases for litigation, you may still be hoping to settle. At your direction, your attorneys may utilize any of a variety of methods to assist you in trying to reach agreement, as you continue to fight with and threaten each other.

As you work towards an adversarial negotiated settlement, you may want to consider the following:

How are cases settled adversarially?

Most typically by negotiating a written Settlement Agreement, with drafts and requested revisions going back and forth between attorneys. Sometimes both attorneys and both parties willingly come together, amicably and professionally, and hash it all out in a four-way settlement meeting to reach agreement as to the final terms.

In other cases, the only way to get all four of you together, is for one of the attorneys to arrange to depose either you or your spouse. Then, after you are all in one room, the attorneys may try to work things out. If you are all successful, the terms of your Agreement will be read into the record before a court reporter, and you will each affirm that Agreement under oath. A proper document will then be prepared at a later date, for you and your spouse to endorse.

Settlement can also be brought about by both adversarial attorneys and both parties working together in one room with a neutral mediator to help with the negotiations, and to help keep everyone calm and polite. Having pastry in the room can help too.

For some issues, such as the division of furnishings and household items, you may each agree, at your lawyers' suggestion, to allow an arbitrator to make a binding decision as to who gets what, and to help you divide the family photos.

Another way to reach agreement is by hiring a retired judge to go back and forth between two different rooms, with you and your attorney in one room, and with your spouse and his or her attorney in another. By using his or her stature, and the provision of evaluative information, that mediator may be able to encourage you both, either gently or not so gently, to reach a settlement.

Occasionally settlement can occur through the utilization of a neutral case evaluation program, conciliation program, mediation program, or other alternative dispute resolution service offered by the courts.

If you, your spouse and your respective attorneys all want to fight and threaten each other towards settlement, you can certainly find a way to do so.

What can I do if my case isn't settling?

If your case can settle, it should. If it isn't settling, you have three basic options:

1. Modify your offer to move closer to your spouse's position, or

2. Maintain the in-limbo *status quo* and do nothing, or

3. Ask for what you want in court.

In other words, even if you try to show your spouse that the relevant law supports your position, you can't make your spouse settle. Your spouse may believe that the law supports what he or she wants more strongly than what you want. Or your spouse may simply want you to just give up and settle for whatever he or she feels like handing you, or taking away from you.

Your spouse may refuse to even tell you what he or she is willing to offer, because he or she wants to put you through the expense and stress of a trial, and would rather spend money on an attorney before giving money to you. Some people will cut off their nose to spite their face.

If I want to settle, but my spouse is not offering a reasonable settlement, do I have to prepare for trial?

Probably. Your spouse may only settle if it looks like you will get what you want in court, and he or she is tired of the litigation, or is tired of paying attorney's fees. You may have to prepare your case for trial, and put your case in the best possible posture, for your case to settle favorably. Your spouse may call your bluff. If it looks like your case is weak, and if you haven't taken all the proper steps to be able to prove your case, your spouse is more likely to refuse to settle, and to force the case to trial. Unfortunately, taking all the steps necessary to put your case in the best possible light may be a very expensive process.

If my spouse isn't reasonably trying to settle, what should my attorney and I be doing to prepare the case for court, or to work towards a more favorable settlement?

First, your attorney should probably conduct discovery. This means he or she will send out to your spouse Interrogatories, and a Request for Production of Documents, to obtain information and documents from your spouse, possibly along with a Request for Admissions. A request to update this discovery should also be made just prior to trial.

Important adverse third party witnesses may need to be deposed, so you can ascertain what they plan on saying against you in court. Perhaps third party subpoenas for documents should be served on banks, and on your spouse's employer, to obtain financial and retirement information not provided by your spouse. You may need to employ the services of a certified fraud investigator, to find out where your spouse has been hiding assets. Custodians of Records may need to be subpoenaed for trial, so the documents can be admitted into evidence over a hearsay objection.

The house may have to be appraised, and if there is no stipulation as to a value for the house, the appraiser may have to be hired to testify in court. All of your other expert witnesses, and your non-expert lay witnesses, must be designated, and all of your exhibits must be listed. You may need to prepare Property Exhibit Schedules, and a trial note-book. The testimony for all witnesses, including you, must be prepared. You do not want to look like a deer caught in the headlights when your spouse's attorney cross-examines you. You should understand all of the statutory factors as to which you will give testimony.

Perhaps a Motion for Alternative Valuation date regarding a marital asset that your spouse wasted should be timely filed. Your attorney must also timely make any proper objections to your spouse's list of exhibits, or the objections may be waived.

Make sure your attorney has a plan, and is working towards some sort of a resolution. To learn more about the litigation process, please see Chapter 14 of this *Guide* entitled *What Happens if We Go to Court?*

If we're heading for court, is it still possible for the case to settle before trial?

Yes. Cases often settle just before the trial date. Some courts will even require participation in some form of alternative dispute resolution process, as a last attempt to settle, before the court will even let the case be tried. To increase the chances of settlement, your attorney should be communicating with the other attorney, and should be making an effort to resolve the case, instead of just letting it go to trial.

In the meantime, you need to be communicating with your attorney, and you need to know exactly what everyone is supposed to be communicating about. How are the assets valued? How is child support calculated under the child support guidelines? What is fair? What is the court likely to do? What does the law say? Whose case is stronger?

Before you head off to court, make sure you know the exact monetary value of, and exactly what you are fighting about, along with just how much money you will spend to litigate the case, so you can evaluate whether or not what you are fighting for is even worth the cost of the fight.

Does a settlement before trial mean "settling for less?"

Sometimes. If your attorney never prepared the case, chances are he or she probably figured you couldn't pay for a trial, and that your case would simply settle for the best the other side would offer just before the scheduled trial date. If your case was never properly prepared, your attorney will tell you that you will just have to agree to whatever your spouse feels like handing you.

The other attorney may not have prepared either. Did they both know the case would never be tried, and that in the end they would just each simply tell you and your spouse what to settle for? Maybe. Did you? Maybe not.

If you are serious about litigating, the other side will know it. You will pay the fees required to do the work necessary, and that work will be done. Then, if settlement occurs, it is just a bonus, and you are spared the attorney's fees for the actual final hearing.

Is God allowed in the courtroom?

No.

Constitutional principles prohibit the court from making any rulings regarding religion. The court will not decide whether, how much of, or which religion your child may be exposed to. Or which religious dietary, hair, dress, or other requirements may or may not be appropriate for your child. God and religious beliefs are usually barred from the courtroom during divorce proceedings. If they need to be resolved through litigation, these issues must usually be presented to the court in a different context, such as whether or not a specific act, cast in nonreligious terms, is in a child's best interests.

However, if you and your spouse wish to address religious or spiritual matters, you are free to do so outside of court. Even in the context of negotiating a settlement agreement in an adversarial manner, the two of you may include provisions in an agreement which you both agree to honor. But if one of you chooses to ignore those provisions, the court may be powerless to enforce them. The judge is not God. Judges enforce legal matters. It's up to God to enforce the rest.

Just as in negotiated out-of-court settlements, in the mediation and collaborative settings you and your spouse also have the ability to address religious and spiritual beliefs, if you choose to do so. You may wish to specifically seek the services of a faith-based mediator, or the services of a faith-based collaborative attorney. You may even choose to actively conduct the proceedings in a spiritual or in a religious way. You would only be limited by the knowledge, expertise, willingness and comfort level of your mediator or collaborative attorneys.

If you find professionals who are respectful of the manner in which you wish to proceed, the efforts to dissolve your marriage are only bounded by your imagination, and by the bounds of the law. Your final Agreement will still be enforced only within the confines of the court's abilities, but it may very well be that if the process is conducted in a meaningful way, you will each be more likely to abide by the results. But be careful the candles don't set off the sprinklers in your mediator's or attorney's office.

Are there advantages to trying to settle from the outset, as opposed to settling only after we have each positioned ourselves for a trial?

Yes. In a perfect world, if you are eventually going to wind up settling, everyone should know it and just settle from the get go. Why waste your money on lawyers? Too bad you're not living and divorcing in a perfect world.

But if you are both reasonable and rational people, and are willing to reasonably settle everything outside of court, you can get creative. You can make temporary agreements and partial agreements. You can free up some money without prejudice to a final resolution. You may refinance or sell a house before all the issues are resolved, and then distribute some of the proceeds to establish new residences. You may start dividing up the investment accounts before everything is in writing. Perhaps you will experiment with custody arrangements, to find out what works best for each of you and for the children. You can pay support without the initial amount being considered some sort of precedent.

If you try to work it out, you can make it work for you.

Okay, if we all want to settle right from the start, how do I pick a mediator, or a collaborative attorney?

Chapter Five

HOW DO I CHOOSE A FAMLY LAW MEDIATOR?

Just as there are all sorts of lawyers out there, there is also a great variety of mediators to choose from. You won't find just the right professional to guide you through this important part of your life if you don't know what to look for, or what to look out for. The type of mediator you will hire will determine the quality and expense of your mediation experience.

You may have simple and limited issues to resolve, or your case may be more complex. You may settle aspects of your case in stages, or you may settle the entire case all in one process. You may have a high asset divorce, or your divorce may be more about emotion. You need a mediator qualified and competent to help you with your particular situation.

Take out that highlighter or pen, and mark up those points listed below which you want to ask about when you go to interview mediators.

Mediators may have any one or more of the following styles, approaches, characteristics or qualifications:

- facilitative, evaluative, directive, transformative, faith-based or informative,

- trained or untrained,

- lawyer; or non-lawyer therapists, financial planners and religious authorities,

- court-certified or uncertified,

- pair mediators who comediate, usually one male and one female,

- mediators who like to reframe and restate what you are each saying, and who want you to direct the process,

- mediators who list your concerns in magic marker on big sheets of paper, and tape them up all around the room,

- mediators who use magic markers on big flip charts set on easels, which charts you may wind up staring at instead of looking at each other,

- mediators who sit behind a desk, who can run child support guideline calculations, and source of fund calculations for separate interests in hybrid property, on their computers for you,

- purely facilitative mediators, who say if you didn't think of and raise an issue all by yourselves, it can't be important to you,

- purely facilitative mediators, who believe that if the mediator raises "new" issues, the mediator is improperly interfering with your self-determination,

- facilitative mediators who want you each to also use individual lawyers to tell you what to mediate, and to point out all the little holes in your Mediated Agreement,

- informative mediators who will tell you what you need to talk about, and who will provide you with a list of topics for you to consider,

- evaluative mediators who, upon request, will neutrally assess the strengths and weaknesses of your positions if you were to go to court, which may help you in deciding on your own how to resolve your case,

- retired judges doing evaluative mediation as a second career, who may engage in a sort of shuttle negotiation between your lawyer and your spouse's lawyer, as you and your spouse each sit next to your respective attorneys in separate rooms and the lawyers do most of the talking,

- uncertified or untrained lawyer mediators, who may actually be doing a sort of directive assisted negotiation bordering on improper dual representation, and not really mediation,

- mediators who will let you each have your own lawyers present in the room during the mediation, and those who don't see the need unless you are already in litigation,

- mediators appointed by the court to help only with custody and support, who have no authority to help you with the interrelated property issues,

- retired government employees or retired government lawyers who can provide valuable mediation services in certain cases, but who may know very little about complex or high asset divorce cases,

- lawyer mediators who actually practice family law and litigate, and lawyer mediators who don't litigate,

- lawyer mediators admitted to practice law in a state other than the state whose laws apply to your case,

- mediators trained in financial planning, who will try to help you come up with a financial plan for the future, but whose conduct may be bordering on improper dual representation,

- non-lawyer mediators, who are not qualified to give you much legal information about the legal process in which you are squarely involved,

- attorney mediators who may be qualified to give you legal information, but who are not comfortable doing so, because they are afraid of unethically advising you,

- attorney mediators who will insist that you become fully informed as to the legal principles surrounding the legal issues you are deciding upon, and who will give you lots of legal information,

- mediators who draw up bullets of "agreements" in a "Memorandum of Understanding," which you then have to take to a lawyer who will draw up an actual binding contract,

- mediators who say they're only a "mere scrivener" for what you say, and who shudder at the thought of adding "legalese" to your legal document,

- non-lawyer mediators who will draft a Memorandum of Understanding, and then if you sign that, won't tell you whether or not that document became a binding contract, because they feel that to do so amounts to improperly giving you legal advice,

- attorney mediators who will prepare a binding Mediated Agreement, including all of the necessary standard boilerplate language which protects you both, and

- attorney mediators who will fully inform you both as to the intricacies of your private and military retirement plans, and who will prepare agreed upon language for pension court orders for you to email to the attorney who will file the divorce case.

Regardless of personal style, each and every mediator conducting his or her practice ethically, and within the appropriate parameters, is a boon to the community. All mediators take the time, and put forth the effort that judges will not, to help you to craft a result tailored to your particular needs. The services which the mediator can provide to you will help you to resolve your disputes in an amicable and respectful way. So, to start the search for the best mediator for you, ask some of the general questions set forth below.

Do I need a trained or certified mediator?

States offer various guidelines for training and experience, and provide oversight for the certification and ongoing recertification of individuals as mediators. However, state certification may not be required of an individual who wants to provide mediation services. Your state may let anyone hang up a sign offering mediation services, with no requirement for initial training or certification, and with no oversight for ongoing training or recertification.

Your pastor, rabbi, Imam, brother-in-law or mutual friend can try to help you through your divorce, and could even charge you for their services. But consider this: if your state requires hairdressers and mechanics to be licensed to work on your hair and car, don't you think it might be appropriate for the person helping you to make permanent decisions about your children, support, debt, house, retirement and other property, to know what he or she is doing?

If you want to mediate in a language other than English, or if you can't find a mediator who understands the cultural issues important to you and to your family, you may seek out a diplomatic, unbiased member of your community to help you get started. However, since your divorce will have to deal with legal issues, and ultimately with a divorce court order, if you do not use a certified mediator, at least do not sign anything until you have had an attorney on your side only review the document.

Can I use a mediator who was appointed by the lower court to resolve temporary custody, visitation and support matters, to help settle all the final divorce issues?

If you have filed for temporary custody, visitation and/or support, many courts will refer your case to mediation with a certified mediator who may or may not be a lawyer. That individual is appointed to help you only with those matters within that court's jurisdiction, and only as to those matters raised by your pleadings. The mediator may have no authority to help you work out what you will do with your debt, house, retirement and other assets. The mediator will be able to draw up an Agreement which will be filed with the court, resolving your temporary support, custody and visitation case. However, that Agreement may or may not also work for the later divorce suit, which case may be in a different court.

If your mediation is largely concerned with custody and visitation matters, and if the property and support issues are not complex or are nonexistent, there are many dedicated professionals working with the courts who will provide caring and competent assistance to you. These individuals are trained, certified and monitored, and are largely involved in mediation because they are motivated by a desire to help people in need. They don't always get paid a whole lot by the state, and are not looking to make money off of the breakup of your family. They may be able to help you in some matters.

But if your divorce case involves a house or retirement assets, or if your case is even more complex, you will probably want to draw up a comprehensive Property Settlement Agreement. Court-appointed mediators may be restricted from mediating property matters, and non-lawyers can not draft binding contracts, since they are prohibited from engaging in the unauthorized practice of law. You will have to hire a lawyer to draw up your Agreement. You also may not want to settle your case in a piecemeal fashion, if the custody and support matters are intertwined with the debt, house and other matters. You may need more than what the courts can provide to you at low cost.

Do I need an attorney mediator?

Your divorce Agreement will probably be the most important document you will ever sign. That Agreement will be incorporated into your divorce case, and will become a binding court order. The document needs to be drafted by a lawyer, since non-lawyers are prohibited from practicing law. If a non-lawyer mediator helps you to work out your differences, and then writes up a (quite possibly) nonbinding "Memorandum of Understanding" listing bullet points of agreement, you will still need a lawyer to turn that document into a legally enforceable contract. That new attorney may tell you that you have to start all over, because you didn't properly consider all the legalities.

If your mediator can't or won't give you sufficient legal information, you will have to hire an attorney to give you that information during the mediation process. Once you are informed, you may realize that some of the positions you initially took in the mediation hurt you. Did you think you were not entitled to any of the increased equity in the marital home which was titled solely in your spouse's name throughout the marriage? Did you think that just because a business your spouse created during the marriage is only in your spouse's name, that you weren't entitled to ask for some of the value of that business? Did the non-lawyer mediator remain silent, or hint that you should ask a lawyer about those issues, since the mediator was more concerned about not appearing biased or about improperly giving advice, than about informing each of you as to exactly what the law is?

If your spouse says that he or she will pay the $30,000 in joint credit card debt, wouldn't you want a lawyer mediator to ask you whether or not you want to include language in your Agreement addressing the payment of that joint debt if your spouse dies? Or a mediator who will discuss with you whether you wish to make it harder for, or try to prohibit your spouse from, discharging that obligation in bankruptcy and sticking it with you? Wouldn't you want a mediator who will ask you if you want to include language in your Agreement requiring your spouse to pay you back, plus the tax consequences to you, if a bankruptcy discharge is obtained by your spouse, and you then have to pay off the debt your spouse promised to pay in order to protect your credit rating? And who will then draft language regarding Domestic Support Obligations under the Bankruptcy Abuse Prevention and Consumer Protection Act for you, and who will include that language in a binding enforceable Agreement?

One way or another, whether you receive the information from a lawyer mediator or from an attorney on your own behalf, you need to know the law.

If I use an *attorney* mediator, should that person also be *certified,* or trained in mediation?

Attorneys who are not certified by the state to provide mediation services, or who are not trained in mediation, may not actually be mediating, and you may not even know it. They may not know it either. Attorneys are so used to telling everyone what to do, and are so used to giving everyone their sage legal advice, that those untrained or uncertified in mediation may approach the resolution of the issues defining your life as if it is all about them and what they think you should do from a legal perspective, and will not really consider what you feel and what you want. They may improperly and unethically advise you, and just "tell you both what you should do." They may not care about what you both want to do, especially if they believe a court would not order the result you want and are trying to create. Lawyers are also so used to negotiating, that an untrained lawyer mediator may simply put you and your spouse in different rooms, and may then just engage in facilitating your negotiations.

So how do I choose a mediator?

Most states maintain a computerized listing of all court-certified mediators, which can be searched by locality. Nonprofit mediation centers offer mediation services in many locales, sometimes in conjunction with the courts. Look in the online phone book, and make inquires with the court clerks. Check out www.divorcenet.com. Talk to friends who went through mediation. Call up the offices of a few mediators, and talk to the person who answers the phone about the services that mediator provides. Set a few appointments. Go interview mediators.

Ask how many sessions it usually takes that mediator to reach a resolution in most cases. If you are serious about settling, it should usually take only a few two-hour sessions. How much would that cost?

Will the mediator give you legal information? Lots of it, or just a little?

What is the mediator's style? Will the mediator show you all the arguments that the lawyers on both sides could make, so you and your spouse don't have to argue with each other, and you each get to hear just how you would sound in court? Will the mediator provide you each, right in front of the other, with the legal information attorneys separately representing you would give to you, so you each get an idea of what your spouse is perhaps being told and believes?

Will there be a binding enforceable contract at the end of the process? Will the mediator provide you each with the legal information which individual lawyers would provide you, if they were to review that Agreement before you sign? Will your mediator provide you each with sufficient legal information, such that you wouldn't hear much if anything new from an attorney reviewing the draft Agreement on your own behalf later on, that you weren't made aware of during the mediation?

Does the mediator charge you to do a "rolling draft" of an Agreement? Why is that necessary? Is it really? Are evening and weekend appointments crucial? Cost? Location? Results?

After you find a mediator with whom you are comfortable, give the process a try.

Chapter Six

HOW DO I CHOOSE A COLLABORATIVE DIVORCE ATTORNEY?

Even if you utilize the services of an attorney mediator who can draw up a binding settlement contract, that attorney can not file your divorce suit in court. Lawyers are ethically prohibited from representing both sides of a dispute simultaneously, even if both parties sign a waiver, and want to "use the same lawyer." You just can't. Attorneys are ethically prohibited from engaging in dual representation.

In the end, an attorney will have to file a divorce suit in court, and ethically it can't be a lawyer who mediated your case. You or your spouse may also need a separate lawyer to prepare a pension order for entry in the divorce case, or a qualified domestic relations order addressing retirement issues, if the mediator did not prepare the language for the order as part of the mediation.

If you each want "your own" attorney to help you settle your case without going to court, instead of using a mediator and then hiring an attorney to file the divorce suit, you can each agree to hire two attorneys to settle your case from the get-go, and to then file and finalize the now uncontested divorce for you. You each hire separate attorneys to do a collaborative divorce case, and to be with each of you from start to finish.

Through a series of four-way meetings, you will all sit down together to work out all the financial and other issues surrounding the dissolution of your marriage, and at those meetings you will address the concerns involving the restructuring of your family.

Collaborative organizations may maintain online directories of trained collaborative attorneys, searchable by locality. Take a look on the internet, and take a look in the phone book. Check out www.collaborativepractice.com, which is the website for the International Academy of Collaborative Professionals, and www.divorcenet.com.

Interview potential attorneys. Does the attorney understand your goals? What sort of collaborative approach does the attorney take? Does the attorney want the process to be so "transparent" that the attorney will not even give you any advice or information unless your spouse is present and listening also? Does the attorney want a whole team involved in the divorce effort, to include coaches for each of you, a child therapist and a financial specialist, all sitting at the table together, with no confidentiality or only limited confidentiality between each of you and all of the team members? Will the attorney also utilize written and email communications back and forth, or will the attorney insist that all communication be face to face? Does the attorney use flip charts at meetings, or simply take notes? Does it matter to you either way?

If your collaborative attorney tells you that the collaborative model he or she uses *requires* the use of "coaches" for both you and your spouse, along with a mental health professional to represent the interests of your child or children during the process, understand that you are free to seek the services of other collaborative attorneys who will let *you* decide upon which collaborative model you wish to utilize. While the collaborative experience may be more satisfying when neutral mental health professionals are used, you may not be able to afford a Lexus divorce. A Honda may also get you to your destination, at significantly less cost. Not everyone needs or can pay for heated leather seats in these difficult economic times.

Does the attorney seemed concerned largely about the "process," and less about the substance, insisting on "briefings," "debriefings" and on the preparation of "Agendas" and "Minutes?" Does the Representation Agreement you are asked to sign include language allowing the attorney to talk all about your private case at collaborative trainings, and at collaborative seminars? Will the attorney take a more minimalist approach, to help keep the costs, effort and time down as low as possible?

Is one approach any better than the other, or does the success of the effort depend more on the attorneys and on you, than on the specifics of how the process is conducted? Or are all the specifics about the "process" what actually make collaborative divorce satisfying and successful?

While mediation is becoming a more commonplace method of resolving divorces, collaborative divorce is still relatively new. The collaborative community is still finding its way in the land of alternative dispute resolution. Trained lawyers who will handle collaborative divorces are showing as large a variety of approaches as do traditional adversarial lawyers, and as do mediators. Just as in choosing a mediator, or in choosing an attorney for your negotiation or litigation, when choosing a collaborative attorney, make sure you are comfortable with that attorney, with his or her approach to resolving your case, and with his or her level of service and attentiveness. Is the attorney accessible? If you are unable to communicate effectively with your attorney, your attorney will be unable to communicate your desires effectively to the opposing party.

Once you have chosen both an approach, and a legal professional to help you down the path you have chosen, it is time to start down that path, one step at a time.

Start making appointments.

⚭

Chapter Seven

DO I NEED OTHER PROFESSIONALS TO ADVISE ME DURING THE DIVORCE PROCESS?

Financial Specialists

Whether you are litigating, negotiating, collaborating or mediating, you may need to involve a financial analyst in the process to value certain assets, and/or to make recommendations as to the division of those assets. Unless they are properly trained, lawyers are not financial advisors. And mediators are ethically prohibited from giving advice. Your attorney or mediator may recommend that you meet on your own, or together jointly with your spouse, with an appropriate financial specialist to inform you, and to help generate financial options.

Have you thought about the following? Perhaps a spouse who can't refinance the entire mortgage on the former marital home, plus the amount to buy out his or her spouse's share, may consider a trade-off of other assets. But are future pension dollars worth the same as present home equity dollars? What if the home is sold more than three years after the separation, and the proceeds divided? Will you or your spouse be hit with capital gains taxes if you or your spouse didn't mainly live in the house for two out of the five years just before it was sold? Should each of you have to bear the costs of future sales commissions, or the closing costs for a refinance if the house is refinanced in one name, and the other person receives payment for his or her interest in the home? Should the cost of the interest paid to the bank to buy out one spouse be considered? Can or would a judge deduct those costs?

Other tax consequences should also be examined. A mutual fund worth $50,000 that used to be worth $100,000 may be more valuable than a mutual fund worth $50,000 that used to be worth $10,000, because there will be capital gains taxes on the latter, but not on the former. A Roth IRA worth $20,000 is more valuable than a standard IRA worth $20,000. You may wish to divide your stock accounts, instead of cashing them out and dividing the proceeds, in order to avoid capital gains taxes.

Spousal support is included in income, and is taxable to the recipient, whereas child support is not. Are there IRS rules of which you should be aware if you agree to call certain payments spousal support, but the IRS thinks they are really child support? Could the IRS hit you with back taxes, penalties, late fees and interest if it decides a payment you called spousal support and deducted really is considered to be child support under the IRS regulations, and you didn't pay enough tax? If spousal support payments graduate downward more than $15,000 from the second year to the third, might the IRS recapture that alimony, and require you to include in your income in the third year part of the alimony payments you previously deducted?

Should you delay a final divorce hearing by agreement, so the marriage lasts a full ten years, and a spouse may then be eligible for higher Social Security payments? Should you delay so the marriage lasts at least ten years overlapping with military service, so the former spouse can receive direct retirement pay from the Defense Finance and Accounting Service, or "DFAS?" Should you delay the divorce so at least twenty years overlap with military service, so as to allow for even more benefits to the servicemember's spouse?

Do you know how to value part-marital and part-separate stock options that are not fully vested? Can a value be placed on a defined benefit pension plan annuity? What is a Qualified Domestic Relations Order, or "QDRO?" Why do you need a QDRO to divide a defined contribution plan like a 401k, 403b or 401a account, when you don't need a QDRO to divide an IRA, and can't use a QDRO to divide a federal Thrift Savings Plan, or "TSP" account?

Can you offset the values of defined contribution plans and IRAs, so you will only need to pay a lawyer to draft one QDRO instead of multiple QDROs? Can you do the whole net transfer from one large IRA instead, so you don't even have to do a QDRO, and can just use a joint Letter of Instruction? Why do the federal government and military not use QDROs? What is a Court Order Acceptable for Processing, or "COAP?" What is a state Approved Domestic Relations Order, or "ADRO?"

Does the marital estate include an executive nonqualified retirement plan, such as a Supplemental Executive Retirement Plan, (SERP), a 412i Plan or a Section 162 Executive Bonus Plan? Do these plans have different tax ramifications than do qualified plans?

Should you undertake the cost to seek the services of a forensic accountant, or the services of a certified fraud investigator, to ferret out hidden assets secretly transferred by your spouse during the marriage? Would it help you to employ the services of a Certified Financial Planner, (CFP), with experience in the divorce process, or the services of a Certified Divorce Financial Analyst, (CDFA), to evaluate your current needs and your future long-term needs, to help you plan a budget and to recommend an allocation of the marital assets? Some CFPs and CDFAs have also received training in mediation and/or in collaboration, and can become an integral part of those processes. Is it a bad idea to just use your family's or business' Certified Public Accountant, or "CPA," who may be biased towards the higher wage earner?

If you don't know the answers to the above questions, you should be nervous. The questions set forth above are only a small sampling of the questions enumerated in Chapter 8 of this *Guide*, entitled *What Exactly has to Be Resolved?* Make sure you know the right questions to ask, and then make sure you get the right answers from the right professionals. The better informed you are, the better a result you will achieve.

Retirement Benefits Analysts

You or your spouse may have retirement benefits, or may be entitled to a portion of the other's retirement benefits. Defined Benefit Plan. Pension. Annuity. Federal Civil Service Retirement System, or "CSRS." Federal Employees Retirement System, or "FERS." FERS Special. Central Intelligence Agency Retirement & Disability System or "CIARDS." State Department. Foreign Service. World Bank. Military. State pension plans. County pension plans. Private pension plans. Separate interest approach. Shared interest approach. Pre-retirement survivor benefits. Post-retirement survivor benefits. Refund of Employee Contributions. Concurrent Disability Payments. Concurrent Retirement and Disability Payments.

Defined Contribution Plan. 401k. 403b. 401a. TSP. VIP Voluntary Investment Program.

What is a QDRO? A COAP? An ADRO? Do I need one to divide an IRA? What is a Qualifying Court Order for a military pension? Is there a cost to elect survivorship benefits? Who pays that cost? And how, if at all, do Social Security benefits fit into all of this, and if they don't, are there certain legal arguments that could be made if one spouse will not receive Social Security and one will?

What happens to the benefit if the private company is purchased by a successor corporation, or goes bankrupt? What is a Plan Administrator? What is a "marital share?" Should our Agreement or the judge define the numerator of that fraction? Can I begin to collect benefits when I am eligible to retire, or when my spouse is eligible whether or not he or she actually does retire? What if there is a retirement based on a disability? Can loans be taken out from a retirement plan?

What if the government plan is converted from one type to another? Are the last three years of salary important, or the highest three? If I, the spouse of the federal employee, remarry before age 55, can I still keep my share of the government pension if my spouse and I agree? But will I lose my right to be maintained as survivor beneficiary, and my right to indefinite health coverage under the Federal Employees Health Benefits (FEHB) program if I had otherwise been eligible? Can survivorship rights be terminated and then reinstated?

Can a value be placed on an annuity? Who is qualified to conduct a pension appraisal? Can contributions to a retirement plan be refunded, emptying the plan? How valuable then would any survivorship rights be?

What if the military does not receive a survivor beneficiary designation within one year of entry of a divorce decree awarding that benefit? What is 20-20-20? 20-20-15? 10? 5? What is direct pay pursuant to the Uniformed Services Former Spouses' Protection Act? Does it matter if the military retirement occurs while on reserve duty, or if the retirement is from active duty? What are creditable service points? Months of creditable service? Good year of service? What is the Defense Finance and Accounting Service, or "DFAS?" What is a Survivor Benefit Plan, or "SBP?" Reserve Component SBP? Deemed election? At what age for the servicemember can a survivor beneficiary designation be made? If a servicemember becomes eligible for and receives disability payments in the future, would that reduce the other spouse's share of the disposable retired pay?

Whether you litigate or settle, you must know what questions to ask. A good retirement benefits analyst can answer all of the above questions in his or her sleep, and will raise a host of other questions which you hadn't even thought of, for you to consider and address. Address them.

Mental Health Professionals

If you or your children are struggling emotionally, you need a therapist. If you have a substance abuse problem, you need treatment. If you have mental health problems, you need treatment and probably medication. If the family relationships are in trouble, you could benefit from the help of a family therapist, parenting coordinator or child specialist. Follow the recommendations of the professionals.

If you are in custody litigation, your lawyer may want to find an expert who will tell the judge that your child would be better off with you than with your spouse. Your spouse may go find an expert also. However, many therapists will not testify in court in a custody suit, because they feel that to do so jeopardizes the child's trust in the therapist, and the child will no longer be forthcoming if the therapist blabs everything the child said to the judge and to the child's parents. The doctor-patient relationship is compromised when confidentiality is broken, and will never be the same.

Medical records and testimony may not even be admissible in court by law for privacy reasons, even if the therapist possesses vital information which should be relevant to a proper custody determination. You may instead ask the judge to order your spouse to participate in family counseling, and to follow the recommendations of the counselor, to better understand the problems the children are having and to improve communication.

You or your spouse may ask for a custody evaluation. But before you plunk down the hefty fee for a barrage of psychological tests and meetings, ask if the evaluator will make a clear decision and recommendation in the end as to which of you should have primary physical custody, or if almost all reports conclude with something like, "the children would benefit from maximized contact with each parent, and from improved communication between all parties." If that is the case, the family therapist may be more useful.

If you are trying to settle, it may help guide your decision-making to receive input from a neutral third party. Some mental health professionals have received formal training in mediation or in the collaborative process. Family therapists, parenting coordinators and child specialists should also be able to help with parenting issues if you are negotiating or litigating. That professional may open your eyes to problems the children are experiencing, and may provide assistance to the family which judges won't provide if you go to court.

Your divorce will cost money to obtain. Spend some of that money to help your children deal with the situation you and your spouse have created for them. They did not choose to be a part of a two-home family, and are the most important assets of the marriage. Help them to become assets to society, and not victims of your divorce. And don't forget to take care of yourself too.

Valuators

Whether you are litigating or trying to settle, you may need an appraiser to appraise your house. If you are looking to offset a future interest in a defined benefit pension plan by a lump sum payment or credit, you need a pension appraiser. If your marital estate includes a business, you may need a business valuator to conduct a proper business valuation to determine the intrinsic value of that business, and to determine what if any portion may be attributed to personal goodwill of only separate and of no marital value.

If you go to court, the judge may not, however, listen to evidence of the fair market value of your home furnishings, which furnishings are eloquently referred to in the family law community as "pots and pans." The court will hear testimony regarding IRAs, CDs, relatively small bank accounts and the NADA values of your cars, but will not hear evidence as to the yard sale value of your entire home's furnishings. The replacement values and original purchase costs will probably not be considered relevant in court. So regarding furnishings, if you don't settle, whoever made the original plan, and has the items in his or her possession, may very well wind up keeping them. Get your share of the family photos and of the wine collection early on.

However, perhaps your marital estate includes original artwork, a large gun collection, a highly trained horse, a pedigreed dog which you are breeding or a jewelry collection. If the worth of these valuable items matters, whether you litigate, negotiate, collaborate or mediate, proper values should be obtained. And if you can agree on one expert to do a valuation, you don't have to pay two professionals to value the same assets. It can get expensive.

Rehabilitative Experts

You may want to prove to the judge that your spouse is voluntarily underemployed, or voluntarily unemployed, so you can ask the judge to impute income to him or to her. Unless you have testimony as to the salary for the job your spouse recently quit, or a recent tax return or admissible paystub, you will have to hire someone to come to court and tell the judge just how much money your spouse could make, right now, if he or she went out there and got a presently available job for which he or she is qualified.

You will have to pay for the services of that person. Your rehabilitative expert will have to review your spouse's resume, educational credentials, training and work experience. The expert may want to prepare questions for you to ask your spouse at a deposition. The benefit obtained by enlisting that person's services may or may not be greater than the cost for those services.

Experts can be expensive. Uninformed decisions can be more expensive. The more information you have, the better a result you will achieve, whether through litigation, negotiation, collaboration or mediation. Make sure you are appropriately informed.

Chapter Eight

WHAT EXACTLY HAS TO BE RESOLVED?

*Okay, you have decided you want to "work **it all** out."* So what exactly has to be worked out? <u>Take out that pen or highlighter, and start marking up, underlining and circling all of the points and questions which apply to you below.</u>

1. Custody

What sort of custody arrangement would be best? Shared physical, and joint legal? Joint legal, with the children having a primary residence with one of us? Sole custody to one of us, and visitation for the other? How does one "visit" with one's children, anyway? Do we want to call it a "parenting plan," or a "custodial schedule?" Do we want to try "nesting," keeping the children in the home while we each take turns with them there, and each stay elsewhere while the other is in the home, until we can afford to maintain two real residences?

Are all of these phrases mere semantics, or do they actually mean something? Will our lives be defined by these words, or instead by the actual relationship we each have with our children? Can these words define and curtail that relationship? Can the language we use now set some sort of "precedent" in our case, if one of us decides to relocate out of state in the future?

Do two-home children have more problems than one-home children, or fewer problems than children living with parents who don't get along and who fight? Do the rules have to be the same in each home? Is it permissible for two-home children to be cared for by the same *au pair* in each home under the *au pair* program? Can we share a nanny instead? Just how vital or unimportant is it for the children to have "stability," and a "home base?" How much stability is enough? How much "disruption" is too much? Does the school guidance counselor, or our church, offer group or separate discussion sessions for children struggling with their parents' divorces?

Can we enter into temporary Agreements to try out different custody schedules, to see if we can determine what works best for all of us? How about visitation every other Thursday after school to Monday morning return to school, or every other Friday evening to Sunday evening? Maybe with a Wednesday overnight, or dinner visitation, on the weeks there's no weekend overnight? Or the children spend Monday and Tuesday with one of us, Wednesday and Thursday with the other, and we alternate Friday through Monday, in an equal shared custody arrangement?

Do we need to put in writing that we will share information regarding the children's schooling and medical care? Should we define who can pick the children up from the daycare center, or drive with them? Do we need to put in writing who can choose the daycare or babysitters? Should we mention how we will care for the children on snow days, on teacher work days and when the children are sick? Can either of us obtain a driver's license for our child over the other parent's objection, or a tattoo or body pierce? What if we can't agree on whether our children should date, hold a job or take allergy or ADD or ADHD medication? Can we each take the children to doctors and to therapists? To different ones?

If we go to court, will there be a temporary custody order, and then a final custody order? Is a "final" custody order ever really *final*, or can that order be modified if there is a significant change of circumstances in the future?

2. **Visitation**

Do we want to have the flexibility to simply work out visitation by agreement, or do we want a formal written schedule as a minimum fallback? Should that schedule address weekends? Should we decide how the children will spend all of their holidays? Which holidays? Does that include Halloween? Should we alternate Christmas Eve to noon on Christmas Day between us each year, and divide the rest of the winter break equally? What about special religious days, special family days, spring breaks and summer vacations? If there's a conflict as to our school break or summer proposals, can the choice of one of us have priority in even numbered years, and the choice of the other of us in odd?

Should we address three day weekends, stepsibling birthdays and other special occasions? What's the best way to consider the children's and our birthdays, Mothers Day and Fathers Day? When do the grand-parents see the children? Can the children still attend all of the family reunions? If we will be living very far apart, will we meet halfway? Can the children fly unaccompanied on direct nonstop flights? At what age? Who will pay the costs for visitation travel? Should we mention telephonic, email and text messaging contact in our Agreement? Should we set up a webcam? Should our Agreement address out of state vacation plans, travel insurance and the sharing of an itinerary? Who should be able to hold the passports for the children?

3. **Child Support**

Will there be a periodic monthly child support payment from one of us to the other? How much should that payment be? When should the payment start? Do we prorate the first month? Do we want to base that amount on the child support guidelines? If a state ninety day or other visitation threshold is reached or exceeded, will we apply a lower shared custody support guideline calculation? How is a "day" defined? How is a "half day" defined? Is the legal definition of a "day" gender neutral? Can we correct the bias in how the law was drafted, by agreement? Can the cost for private school be considered by the court? Will the non-custodial parent have to contribute to work-related daycare costs? What about daycare costs for one of us to attend classes, or to go out socially?

Should payments be made by direct pay, by direct deposit, by voluntary wage assignment or by payroll withholding order? Is it advisable to have support paid by military allotment, and not directly, by an active duty servicemember deployed in a high conflict zone, who could go missing? Should payment go through the state child support enforcement authorities? If a petition or motion for support has been filed, would the support obligation be retroactive to the filing date? Could a divorce filing divest a lower court filing, and wipe out any retroactive obligation? Could the divorce court judge make the obligation retroactive to the date of filing in the lower court anyway? Is that relevant to the strategy of the case? What if there are arrears? Exactly what time period do the arrears cover? By when should the arrears be paid? Does the law provide for interest on retroactive back due support?

If my spouse or former spouse does not pay court-ordered temporary child support, what enforcement mechanisms are available to me during the divorce process? Can his or her wages be garnished and tax refund be intercepted and paid to me? Can his or her professional, business or driver's license be suspended under state law? Can suspended or actual jail time be imposed until arrearages are paid in full with interest? Under the federal Personal Responsibility and Work Opportunity Reconciliation Act of 1996, or "PRWORA," can his or her fishing, hunting or other recreational license be suspended and passport be revoked? If I can't find my spouse or former spouse, can the federal parent locator service help me?

4. **Extracurricular Activities**

Could a judge order contribution to payments for swimming, karate, dance, soccer, scouting and for other extracurricular activities and camps? Do we want to address those matters in our Agreement? What about holiday presents, back to school clothes, birthday gifts, computer-related costs, religious education costs, SAT preparation course fees, college application fees, senior year activity fees, driver's education course costs and the costs for a car or for car insurance for a child? What if we can't agree upon the activities in which our child should become involved, or upon how the costs should be allocated? What if my spouse signs our child up for activities on "my days," or won't take our child to the practices for the sports or activities in which I enrolled him or her? Can I lead the scouting group, coach the team, attend the games and go to practices? With my new significant other?

5. **College**

Can a judge order either of us to pay for college? If we agree in writing to pay college costs, could our 30 year old child sue us on the contract to enforce that obligation as a third party beneficiary, and then make us pay for an eight year program, majoring in basket weaving, at the University of the Virgin Islands in St. Thomas? Should we limit our obligations to the instate rate at our state university for tuition, fees, on-campus room and board, books and a reasonable amount for travel, to obtain a four year degree or until age 23, whichever occurs first? Or for eight semesters, unless the program is a five year combined degree program?

If we agree in writing to pay college costs, could one of us discharge that obligation in a bankruptcy? Do we have any educational Section 529 accounts, Uniform Trust for Minors Act (UTMA) or old Uniform Gift to Minors Act (UGMA) custodial accounts, or mutual fund accounts set up for the children's college educations? Should we set them up and obligate ourselves to contribute to them? Who should own them? Can we jointly own a custodial account? Can we agree to purchase a prepaid tuition plan for a very young child when we sell our house?

6. Alimony

Alimony, spousal support and support and maintenance may all mean the same thing.

Temporary, final, permanent, lump sum, defined duration or rehabilitative? Either of us can ask for alimony. The law is gender neutral, and guys can get support too. How much should the payment be? When should it start? Will there be a mutual waiver of spousal support? Should we each complete an Income and Expense Sheet to determine our mutual needs, and the payor's ability to pay? Spousal support is includable in the income of the recipient, and deductible from the income of the payor. What does that mean? What are the statutory factors the judge would consider in awarding alimony, if we were to go to court?

Can we agree that support will only be paid for a specific duration? If we don't go to court, do we want to agree to graduate support downward over time? Upward? Could a judge order that? Do we want to graduate the support downward, by set amounts, for specific time periods? Should spousal support be modifiable, or nonmodifiable? Do we want to make the support modifiable by the court upon request in the future, but with a minimum floor and/or a maximum ceiling?

If we do go to court, is "permanent" spousal support really *permanent*, or could permanent spousal support be reduced or terminated if a significant change in circumstances occurs, such as enough time passing for an employable spousal support recipient to be earning more money? Or could the support be increased if the recipient's health care and prescription costs increase, or if the payor's salary increases? If the payor remarries a spouse who works, or if the payor wins the lottery, does that increased ability to pay mean the ex-spouse could then ask for an increase in support, without demonstrating a valid increased need?

When should support terminate? Would support terminate upon either of our deaths, or upon the remarriage or cohabitation of the recipient, if the payment were ordered by the court? Would the termination occur immediately upon cohabitation, or only after one year of cohabitation? Does the cohabitation have to be in a relationship analogous to a marriage? Can that also include same-sex cohabitation? Can we agree that spousal support will automatically terminate upon cohabitation for a lesser period of time, or if the recipient obtains a job at a certain salary level? What if the cohabitation then ends, or the new job is then lost? Would a terminated support obligation be revived?

What if I don't need alimony right now, but may need it later on? Can I reserve my right to seek spousal support in the future, if I become unemployed or seriously ill? Does state law set forth a presumptive duration for the reservation of alimony, for a period of time equal to half the duration of the marriage? Can the presumptive duration be rebutted, if I am in remission from cancer, or if I didn't work during most of the marriage and we were married for a very long time, or for other reasons?

7. <u>Health Insurance Coverage</u>

Will either of us provide health insurance for the other, or should we each provide our own? Can my spouse drop coverage for me during the next open season, or change to a plan that is not as good? Can he or she just drop the dental or vision plan?

For how long can one of us provide health insurance for the other? What happens when we get divorced? Can I still utilize my ex-spouse's employment-provided health benefits under the Consolidated Omnibus Budget Reconciliation Act, (COBRA), if I pay the employer's portion along with my portion? For how long does COBRA coverage last, and how expensive would it be? Would private health insurance cost about the same, or less? If I have a preexisting condition that may require surgery, would it make sense to pay for the up to 36 months of COBRA coverage, before switching plans?

For how long can the children be covered under the plan? Does or should the coverage include dental, optical and psychological services? Should we each maintain insurance for the children, so we have secondary coverage? Can we each hold insurance cards for the children?

If I am covered for at least one day in the 18 months prior to my divorce, remain unmarried at least until age 55, and am entitled to a retirement benefit of at least $1.00 from my federally-employed spouse, can I remain eligible to participate in the Federal Employees Health Benefits Program, (FEHB), for the rest of my life?

8. <u>Unreimbursed Medical Expenses</u>

Should we each be responsible for paying our own noncovered medical expenses? How would these expenses be allocated for the children, if we were to go to court? Equally? In the guideline percentage after the first $250.00 per child, per calendar year, is paid by the custodial parent? How should we split these costs? Should these expenses include work that is purely cosmetic in nature? Are braces considered cosmetic, or reasonable and necessary? Dental bleaching before the prom? Caps and bridges to correct gaps? What is an Explanation of Benefits Form, or "EOB?" Can the insurance company be ordered to send reimbursement checks to me, instead of to my spouse who carries the insurance, if I pay the bill? What is a Qualified Medical Order?

9. <u>Flex Funds</u>

How should we allocate the dependant care expenses for our children, or the health care expenses we can each claim under our flexible spending accounts? If only one of us has a cafeteria plan, or a flex fund, should the other receive an offset for the tax benefit elsewhere in our Agreement? Do we need to cooperate with respect to who pays and who receives reimbursement for the medical bills, if we wish to maximize and share these tax benefits?

10.   Life Insurance, Disability Insurance and Long-Term Care Insurance

If either of us dies, will the spousal or child support payments stop? Can the one of us who survives afford the added cost to raise the children alone? If we agree to maintain life insurance, who should be named as beneficiary? Can minor children receive life insurance proceeds? Can the parents of the friend my child chooses to live with during his or her senior year in high school, instead of moving out of the school district, petition for the release of those proceeds, and then build an addition onto his or her home to "better accommodate" my child? Do I want a young adult 18 or 19 years of age to receive hundreds of thousands of dollars of life insurance proceeds outright, as named beneficiary, if either of us dies?

What if I name someone I "trust to do the right thing" as beneficiary of the life insurance proceeds, and then that person dies? Does his or her executor have a fiduciary duty to give my money to his or her spouse or children? If I name my X2B as beneficiary directly, because he or she would properly use the money for our children, and then he or she remarries and dies without a Will, does the money go to his or her new spouse?

Should we set up trusts to receive life insurance proceeds, designate trustees to authorize the use of those funds, and set an age by which the children will receive the remaining proceeds of the trusts? Do we want to name the other as trustee, so he or she doesn't have to ask someone else every time the children need something, or do we want a third party to oversee the use of the money?

Should we look into separating a joint term policy, and maybe converting to whole life policies? Can I own a life insurance policy on my spouse's life? If I want to obtain and pay for such a policy, can my spouse be ordered to submit to the physical examination requirement? Can he or she agree to do so voluntarily? Is there a cash value to our insurance policy, of which I should receive a portion?

If spousal or child support is to be paid, and the payor then becomes disabled, will the payments stop? Is it possible to require the paying spouse to obtain a long-term disability insurance policy? Could this be negotiated by agreement?

If I can no longer count on my spouse helping to care for me if I need in-home or nursing home care once I am older, and now that I know I will be on my own in my later years, should I look into purchasing a long-term care insurance policy? How much will that cost? Should that cost be figured into my spousal support request?

11.   **Former Marital Home**

Which one of us will stay in the home until it is sold or refinanced? How do I find out if I can qualify to refinance both the mortgage, and the money I will need to buy out my spouse? If we have a favorable fixed interest rate, can I assume our existing mortgage? Will I have the right to exclusive possession of the home, or can my spouse also enter the home whenever he or she wants? Who will pay the monthly mortgage, homeowner association fees and utility bills? Can we split the mortgage interest deduction? By when should the home be sold or refinanced? What if the person trying to refinance can't qualify by that date?

What should the value be for the buyout? If the person refinancing does not have that money, and has to borrow it, should the cost to pay the interest be considered? Should real estate commissions be deducted from the buyout value? Should there be reimbursement for any post-separation reduction in principle attributable to post-separation mortgage payments? Would the court deduct the cost of a sale when there is a refinance and buyout, or only some of the costs for the refinance? Do we have to do what the court would do, if we settle and prepare our own Agreement?

If one of us takes in a renter, can the other of us try to claim a portion of the rental proceeds? Can we afford to maintain the property? Would we have to bring so much money to the table to sell the property that we need to consider a short sale, a foreclosure or even a bankruptcy? Do we want to try to hold on to the home until we can sell it without incurring a loss? What would the consequences be if one of us dies after the divorce is final, and the home and mortgage are still in both of our names?

If the home is to be sold, should we make some repairs or improvements to the property, before it is listed? How should that cost be allocated? Can some of the costs advanced by one of us be reimbursed from the other's share of the proceeds at closing? How should the list price be determined? Should we have the property appraised? By whom? What if the realtor recommends lowering the list price at some point, and one of us doesn't want to lower the price? Can we agree that a sign be placed in the yard, and a lockbox on the door? Can one of us increase the loans on the property, or utilize a home equity line of credit, before the property is sold? How should the proceeds from the sale be divided?

What if one of us dies before settlement on the property, and we are still married? Do we want the property to go in full to the surviving spouse, or do we want the deceased spouse's share to go to his or her heirs? Should we sign a new Deed conveying the property to ourselves with survivorship rights, just after the divorce is final, so that if one of us dies before the property is sold, the other of us won't then own the property with the deceased person's heirs?

Did one of us make a contribution to the down payment that came from separate, premarital funds? Could the spouse who made that contribution prove to the court's satisfaction that the funds were truly separate, and had not been commingled with marital assets? Should that separate contribution, and perhaps the increase in equity attributable to the contribution, be considered, or would that be inequitable, unfair and unjust? Would the granting of a reasonable return on the separate investment be a more equitable approach, such as applying an appreciation percentage to the separate contribution?

12.   **Household Furnishings and Collections**

How should we divide all of our household furnishings, electronics, computers and exercise equipment? Should the jewelry we each gave to the other be appraised, or can we just agree to each keep our own? What if we purchased a large jewelry collection for the marriage? If it was purchased prior to the ceremony, is the jewelry marital property, or a separate premarital gift? Is the engagement ring separate property, or part of an agreement to marry or stay married? What if the diamond was an heirloom from the groom's side?

How should we divvy up the gun collection, artwork and oriental rugs purchased during the marriage? How would the court view all of our stuff and allocate it? Do we also have to value the other marital and separate property, if we want the court to consider any property items? Would the court even consider how our belongings should be distributed? From what options or methods can we choose to divide these items ourselves?

13. Investment Real Estate, Timeshares and Commercial Property

Should we appraise our investment property? How should that property be divided? Can we share the use of our timeshare, or campsite? Can we agree to bequeath our timeshare to the children somehow? Which one of us should manage the property? Who should pay the mortgage, homeowner association fees, condo fees and/or maintenance fees? Once we are divorced, how important is it that we prepare a new Deed addressing survivorship interests? Can we remove properties from a real estate investment trust?

14. Liquid Assets such as Bank Accounts, IRAs, Certificates of Deposit, Mutual Funds, Annuities, Commodities Accounts, Stocks, Stock Portfolios and Stock Options

How do we place values on our liquid assets? Should we meet with a financial analyst to help us determine those values? How do we divide these assets? Can we offset values, so fewer assets have to be retitled? Do we need special court orders to transfer funds from one IRA to another, or will the final decree of divorce be sufficient to accomplish that transfer, along with a joint Letter of Instruction with a Medallion Signature Guarantee? Can we divide the funds in a SEP IRA, or in an old Keogh plan?

If we cash out and divide a mutual fund account, will there be taxes on any capital gain? If there is a capital loss, can we share the right to carry over that deduction on each of our tax returns, if we file separately? Do we need to look at the basis of each stock, and whether depreciation has been taken in the past, in order to determine the tax consequences of a division?

Is the right to purchase stocks below market value, and to then sell those stocks at market value, under an Employee Stock Purchase Plan, a marital asset? Could a purchase and resale be ordered by the court?

Could we agree to exercise this benefit and share the tax consequences, as a way to find and utilize "free money?"

Are inherited property and gifts from third parties part of the marital estate? What if separate inheritance, or third party gift funds, have been commingled within or deposited into marital accounts? Are the funds then transmuted from separate to marital property?

What strike price is stated on the stock option grant? When do the shares vest? When would the options expire? If we decide to grant the other spouse a right to the proceeds from the exercise of a portion of each grant, should that spouse only receive the proceeds net after all costs and tax liability? Will the exercise of the options increase the holder's tax rate? Should a further adjustment therefore be made after the holder's actual taxes are calculated?

15. Prepaid Tuition Plans, UTMA Custodial Accounts and Section 529 Plans

Who owns the Prepaid Tuition Plan? Can ownership be transferred? Who should control the custodial accounts? Do we have an old Uniform Gift to Minors Act (UGMA) account? Can we now be joint custodians on the Uniform Transfer to Minors Act (UTMA) account? Can either one of us sign for withdrawals? Do we have to agree as to how the money in these accounts can be spent? Should our Agreement state that these funds shall be used for college costs? Could a judge order that? Can we each open Section 529 accounts for each of our children, so we are both able to deduct contributions? How much would we really each then save overall on our yearly state income taxes?

16. Bonds

What should we do about all of the bonds we saved and which the children were given over the years? Should the bonds be cashed in? Can we agree as to their use? Should the value be divided or offset against other assets? Should we divide or offset the current value of the bonds, or the value the bonds will be worth upon maturity? Does it matter from which side of the family the bonds were given? Can we agree to give the bonds to the children, or agree to only use them for the children's benefit? Do the Bar Mitzvah gifts belong to us, or to our child? Can the judge even make an award to either of us in a divorce suit for control over the ownership of our child's property?

17. Royalties

How can we divide book royalties? Could there be further marital rights in print, tape, movie rights, consulting fees, box office, video games, product, toys, action figures, CD's, clothing and licensing agreements in relation to any logo? How can we share the tax consequences? How do we obtain or provide verification of these amounts? Should we also work with a tax attorney and with an accountant?

18. Private, Federal or State Defined Benefit Retirement Pension Plan Annuities and Survivorship Rights

What are all the ins and outs of the retirement plan? How do we divide the plan? What does "marital fraction" mean? Are there pre-retirement survivorship benefits? Post-retirement survivorship benefits? What happens to the survivor beneficiary designation once we are divorced? Can a pension plan be valued, and the lump sum value due one of us be offset by the value of an interest in home equity, or in other assets?

If the Participant of the private (non-government) retirement plan has not yet retired, can the former spouse elect payment under a separate interest approach for a plan covered under the Employee Retirement Income Security Act, (ERISA), whereby the former spouse's share of the accrued benefit is actuarially adjusted to provide a benefit over that spouse's lifetime, rather than over the Participant's lifetime, and where the former spouse could begin to receive payments as soon as the Participant is *eligible* to retire, instead of having to wait until he or she actually *does* retire? Would this enable the former spouse to continue to receive the same level of benefits should the Participant die, unlike if the shared interest approach were applied?

What is the difference between a qualified retirement plan and a nonqualified plan? Does it make any difference to me which type of plan we are trying to divide? Is a defined benefit cash balance plan an annuity, or an account?

Can our attorney mediator explain all of this to us, and draft language we agree upon to use later in the court order that will accompany the divorce decree? Should we also talk to a retirement benefits specialist?

19. Defined Contribution 401k, 403b, 401a and TSP Plans and Survivorship Rights

How would the court divide the retirement accounts that we each earned through our employment? Are there premarital and post-separation separate components to these accounts? Survivor beneficiary designations? Can those designations be changed to third parties while we are still married, if we decide to waive survivorship rights in each other's accounts? Can the designations be changed once we are divorced? Can one of us receive funds outright from one of these plans after the divorce? What would the penalties and tax consequences be for such a withdrawal? Is it better to roll the funds into another tax-deferred account, to avoid penalties and negative tax consequences, using a Qualified Domestic Relations Order, or "QDRO?"

20. Business Interests

Should we have the business valued? How complicated or simple can that process be? How expensive? Will it be necessary for the valuator to review at least the business' general ledger, filed tax returns, reviewed financial statements, all contracts in effect, accounts receivable and due, key man insurance and all employee compensation records? Must all office equipment and any inventory be valued? Should the valuator and each law firm sign a Nondisclosure Agreement? Will it be necessary to obtain a protective order if the business involves government contracts, or possesses other protected information?

Are there certain factors, or assumptions, contained in the valuation methodology, upon which we may disagree? Should we have more than one valuation performed, or agree upon one evaluator? Can we agree if the business is sold within one or two years from our divorce for more than the value we agreed upon, that there be additional compensation? And for each year after that, additional payment of a decreasing percentage of the sale proceeds? What is intrinsic value? Is personal goodwill a separate, non-marital asset? How should we allocate the company name, domain name, website and commercial real estate? How are the tax consequences factored in if stocks have to be sold? If we mediate, and one of us does not make full disclosure, will that nullify and void our Agreement by law?

21. <u>Cars, Boats, Motorcycles, ATVs, Personal Watercraft, Campers and Aircraft</u>

How would the court allocate these items? Should we value them? How? Who has to pay the property tax, insurance and liens? Or slip and hanger fees? Can we decide how to allocate these items in any way we want? Is the court required by statute to consider NADA values for motor vehicles? How and when should our vehicles be retitled? What happens if we don't retitle a jointly owned car, and one of us dies after the divorce? Would the court order a large five year joint car loan at zero percent interest to be paid off immediately? Can we continue the joint car insurance policy if the cars are not garaged together? Will we both remain liable on a joint motor vehicle lease? Should we dispose of our farm equipment at auction?

22. **Pets and Livestock**

Should we discuss, or put in writing, any agreements regarding the sharing and care of our pets? Do we need to? What if one of us goes on a vacation, without the family dog? Can the court order the veterinary or boarding costs to be shared? How does the court view pets? What is a chattel? How would the ownership or value of the pedigreed dogs and cats we breed be determined and awarded by the court? Should we discuss obligating the one of us who keeps our family pet to notify the other of us if the pet needs to be put down? Can a value be placed upon a trained horse, or upon a registered breeding dog or cat? Should we set forth terms governing the use and boarding of our horse in our Agreement? How should we value and divide our farm animals and livestock?

23. **Other Assets**

Does the airline job also provide flight benefits? Can those benefits be considered or allocated in the divorce? Can the equity country club, yacht club, golf club or pool membership be divided? What is it worth? Have we accumulated a lot of frequent flyer miles, and points or rewards for hotel usage? Is there unused earned leave that is worth quite a bit? Is a bonus paid after our separation date, but the right to which was earned prior to the separation, a marital asset? Is a capital loss tax carryover a marital asset?

Is a pending lawsuit a marital asset? Is a recovery from a personal injury lawsuit marital property? Is the entire recovery marital property, including the pain and suffering component, or only those portions of the award attributable to lost wages and medical expenses? What if one of us holds a copyright, patent or ownership of other intellectual property?

Can these assets be divided? Should we jointly inventory the contents of the safe deposit box? What is in there, anyway?

24. <u>Credit Card and Other Debt</u>

Who should pay what? What happens if one of us dies, or files for bankruptcy, and we have joint accounts? If we put all the credit card numbers into our Agreement, will we have to pay a lawyer to prepare a Privacy Addendum to our Agreement, and then redact all of those numbers later on? Can we describe the accounts without stating the account numbers, so we don't have to pay our lawyers to do all that? Who gets to keep the digital photo account, internet account and accompanying email address? Are those debts, or assets?

25. <u>Taxes</u>

How should we file for each year we are still married on December 31st? As married filing jointly, or as married filing separately? Can one of us file as head of household? Will an unfairness occur if we file jointly, and one of us has over-withheld or under-withheld on taxes? Will a joint filing benefit one of us more than the other, if individually we would be in different tax brackets? If we file jointly, how should we divide any refund or further liability? What could happen if the IRS comes after us years later for mistakes we made in a jointly filed return, or for taxes we didn't pay while married?

If we file as married filing separate, or when we are divorced and file as single, who can claim the mortgage interest deduction on our former marital home, and the deduction for the interest paid on our home equity loan? Can we each claim portions of each? Who gets to deduct any capital loss we may have?

Who is entitled to claim the dependency exemptions, deductions and credits for the children? Can that right be transferred if certain requirements are met? What is IRS Tax Form 8332? If we each have shared custody of one child, can we each file as head of household?

26. Divorce Proceedings

Should we decide upon who will file (and pay for) the divorce case after our Agreement is signed? Do we each need a lawyer for the divorce? How do we determine our date of separation? Must that date be corroborated by a third party? Can we use different separation dates for what happened, for what we can prove and for the division of retirement benefits? What is an in-house separation?

Can our Agreement state that the party who does not file the divorce suit will cooperate in getting the divorce, so he or she does not have to be served, and so we each know how the case will proceed? Would a statement in our Agreement to that effect be enforceable, or would such a statement be against some public policy against the facilitation of divorce? Does it matter either way?

Who pays to finalize any retirement orders? Will our mediator explain how the actual divorce process works? Will either of us ever have to go to court if we have settled all the issues, or if the case is uncontested? What is a divorce deposition? What is an *ore tenus* hearing? Is it still possible to have a Commissioner's Hearing for good cause? If we litigate the case, will a new marriage to another be void or voidable if an appeal is filed staying the execution of the divorce decree?

27. Partial, Temporary or Complete Agreement

If we can resolve everything but one or two issues, can we write up an Agreement that resolves those issues, but still allows us to go to court, or to resolve at a later date the things we can't yet agree upon? Can we agree to sell the house, or to use home equity or other assets, subject to argument at trial or in settlement as to credit offsets or reimbursement?

Can we agree to try out different custody arrangements for limited periods of time, to see how well they work?

28. Standard Boilerplate Language

Don't contracts usually contain certain necessary standard language that protects each of us, and which clarifies our intent?

If we were to reconcile, would the Agreement be abrogated under state law? Should we agree that our Agreement would not be nullified by a reconciliation? What if we reconcile, and then separate again? Is our written Agreement still in effect? Could there be a child support arrearage if we separate again after a reconciliation, if a check hadn't been tendered for child support for each month we were together? Can we, or should we, agree to suspend any executory obligations, such as the payment of support, during any reconciliation period? Shouldn't language be included in our Agreement for our protection? Will our mediator include this language in our Agreement?

Can we put language in our Agreement nullifying any Powers of Attorney we may each hold for the other, effective either upon the signing of the Agreement, or upon the filing or completion of a divorce suit? How important are waivers to future claims, and full statements of release? Should there be a blanket waiver of any claims to each other's estate, or do we want to still be able to inherit under each other's Wills, especially under any new Wills prepared after the divorce?

Can our Agreement be modified in the future? How? What if we need to clarify something in our Agreement down the road, such as the value of an asset? If one paragraph of our Agreement is deemed invalid by a judge, does that invalidate the entire Agreement, or are the provisions severable? How many copies should we sign? Under what state's law is the Agreement to be interpreted and governed? When does the Agreement become effective? Do we need to sign the Agreement before a notary public, and initial every page of each copy?

Can We Talk About These Matters by Ourselves?

Yes.

The more you and your spouse can resolve on your own, the less you will each have to pay your attorneys or your mediator. If you can decide together upon some of the issues easily, why pay to chit chat with each other when you are on the clock with the professional, when you can chat over a cup of coffee, or over lunch? Even sitting in a gourmet restaurant would be cheaper than sitting in your lawyer's or in your mediator's office. You can also type up some bullet agreement points to give to your attorney, or to your mediator, so he or she may only have to clarify your intent and flush out all the details with you, before drafting a document.

But if you begin to argue, or are far apart on certain issues, leave those issues alone. Your attorney or mediator is trained to help you work through the tough spots. And whatever you do, do **NOT** argue with each other over these matters in front of your children. To do so is to deliberately inflict hurt, anger, pain and fear, which your child may never overcome or forgive you for inflicting.

However, perhaps one of you does not feel like trying to work it out, and wants to "leave it up to the judge," or wants to "let the lawyers work it all out." If that is the case, understand that the lawyers can spend lots of time quibbling, either in court or out of court, over any one or all of the above questions. They can also dream up even more questions to ask, with lots and lots of letters, phone calls, faxes, emails, revised draft Agreements, settlement meetings and hearings. They won't mind at all. But you may mind all of the Invoices for Professional Services Rendered.

See what you can accomplish on your own first. Start talking.

⚜

Chapter Nine

HOW MUCH LAW DO I NEED TO KNOW?

Okay, I'm accepting the fact that my marriage is over, and I am now involved in the settlement or litigation process. I have made a plan, and am implementing it. I now know what issues need to be resolved. Can I just trust the legal professional to resolve everything to my benefit?

No.

Lawyers and mediators are there to assist **you** in the process. You can't just dump your life in your lawyer's or in your mediator's lap, and ask him or her to "fix it." The attorney advising and guiding you will require you to call the shots and to make decisions, based upon his or her sound recommendations. Similarly, the mediator informing and guiding you will also require you to decide upon the options which you feel are best for your situation.

If you have a lawyer collaborating, negotiating or litigating your case, your lawyer will inform you as to the law and the strength of your positions, and will advise you as to what is in your individual best interests. You then have to decide what you will accept, or how to proceed, based upon your attorney's recommendations, your personal beliefs and needs, the likely response of your spouse, the likely outcome and the financial and emotional costs of protracted litigation.

If you are in mediation, the mediator will inform you and your spouse as to the law, will guide you both in the process, and will offer for your consideration options you hadn't thought of, or of which you were not aware. The mediator will then leave it to you and your spouse to decide upon your options, or may assist you and your spouse in negotiating with each other.

You should be guided somewhat in your decision-making by an understanding of how reasonable or unreasonable your positions are, based upon what would happen if you were to go to court. If you make these decisions based solely on emotion, on your spiritual and religious beliefs, and on your personal feelings of what is right and what is wrong, you may spend a lot of money on litigation, only to be disappointed in the final outcome.

Although those personal feelings may have a role in mediation and in collaboration, and possibly in adversarial negotiation, your personal ideas of fairness may have no relevance in litigation, except as a factor in determining how expensive your case will be if your settlement positions are far afield of how the judge is likely to rule. You could even wind up being ordered to pay some of your spouse's attorney's fees. The judge and the law may not agree with your view of justice.

For example, if your husband of thirty years who is at the height of his earning potential has left you for another woman, or for another man, you may not like hearing that the judge may consider that betrayal to be absolutely irrelevant to your requests for spousal support and for the division of property, under state law. You may spend a whole lot of money on private investigator fees and on attorney's fees, simply to obtain a piece of paper legally stating for the record that your husband found someone he would rather sleep with than you.

You may not want to hear that your involvement in an intimate affair may have a dramatic effect on your ability to obtain spousal support, even if the extramarital relationship began well after the final separation from your spouse. You may also not want to hear that if your spouse walks out on you, a good and dutiful spouse, for no just cause or excuse, he or she is still likely to get half of everything. If you pursue a desertion divorce, you may simply spend a lot of money trying to buy a piece of paper signed by a judge legally announcing to the public that your spouse got tired of you, before you got tired of him or her.

Maybe in the olden days, if your spouse had committed a fault ground for divorce, perhaps he or she would have had to pay all of your attorney's fees, and might not have been awarded any property or spousal support by the court. Nowadays, that may not be the case. Some judges have come to the conclusion that assessing blame for the breakup of the marriage serves merely to increase the conflict between the parties, and that fault can often be assigned to both parties in varying degrees.

However, other judges may feel differently, especially if the fault has had a financial impact on the value of the marital estate. The result is some degree of variability in how the issue of fault is addressed in awarding spousal support, and in dividing property interests. Be sure you find out from local practicing family litigators how your local judges view fault claims.

Can I cooperate with the adultery divorce suit my spouse will file against me, so we have an uncontested fault divorce? If my paramour testifies simply to the occurrence of one act of intimacy during my marriage, and isn't worried about self-incrimination, is this the fastest way for us to get divorced? Does that mean I may be able to remarry before the new baby is born, so he or she is not born out of wedlock?

If I file a divorce suit based on the no-fault grounds of us living separate and apart, but my spouse and I can not agree as to the division of our assets, or as to custody and support, does that mean we have a contested no-fault divorce suit?

Is it true that my abusive, alcoholic husband is still likely to get half of our marital assets? Am I "deserting" my spouse who is violent, and who is openly committing adultery, if he still wants to stay married to me, but his conduct is so intolerable that it is driving me out of the home? What is "constructive desertion?"

If my spouse went on a spending spree just before our separation, knowing we would be divorcing, will I get stuck with half of the debt? What is "waste?" Can the value of our assets be defined as of prior to when my spouse liquidated them? Is it permissible for me to withdraw marital funds for a marital purpose, or for living expenses and/or attorneys fees, after we are separated? Does the answer to that question depend on how much money I am earning?

If my spouse and I have had separate bedrooms for a year, is that sufficient to prove grounds for a no-fault divorce based on living separate and apart? Why not? What else do I have to prove? What level of third party corroboration is necessary? Can we pick one date of separation for the pension calculations, and use another date of separation for the divorce grounds?

What if my spouse is mentally incompetent, or incarcerated? Do I have to pay for an attorney, or for a guardian *ad litem*, for him or her? Can my spouse suffering from a mental health problem, or struggling with a substance abuse problem, even validly enter into a binding Agreement?

If a child was born to me and my spouse prior to our marriage, does the paternity of that child need to be acknowledged or established? What are the legal presumptions and ramifications if my spouse conceives or fathers a child with someone else during our marriage? Can paternity tests be ordered? Should they be? Could I be liable for over 18 years of child support for a child born to my wife prior to the entry of our divorce decree, even though the child is clearly not mine, if that decree did not state that the child was fathered by another?

What if I suspect that one of our children born during the marriage was not fathered by me? Should I ask for a paternity test? Is "the truth" paramount? If a test is not done, will I always view that child differently, or would I still view and treat the child as my own? What is "fatherhood?" Is fatherhood a different concept than biological paternity? Does the mere fact that I want to know the child's true paternity show that I really do not fully view and accept that child as mine? What would "the truth," or the request for a paternity test, do to that child's well-being?

Can my spouse really just up and take the children, and resettle out of the country? Should I try to get a temporary custody order? What is the Hague Children's Convention? To which countries does that treaty apply? Should I notify Immigration and Customs Enforcement, (ICE), if I think my spouse will try to leave the country with our children?

Which state's laws apply in a custody suit, if my spouse and I reside in two different states? What is the Uniform Child Custody Jurisdiction and Enforcement Act, or "UCCJEA?" Will the custody case be heard in the courts of the child's home state, or in the state from which the child was removed? Which state's laws would apply in a support suit? What is the Uniform Interstate Family Support Act, or "UIFSA?"

If I have physical custody of the children, and if I were to die, would custody automatically go to my new spouse, or to my ex-spouse by operation of law? Would a new spouse, who has lived with my children for years, have legal standing to petition for custody as a stepparent after my death? Could he or she argue that it is in my children's best interests not to be uprooted from their step or half siblings, friends, school and support system, to go and live with my ex? If I had physical custody of the children and die unremarried, could the court disregard the designation in my Will for guardian, and award custody to someone else?

If my spouse or ex-spouse who had physical custody of the children in another state were to die, could *anyone* petition for the custody of my minor children upon my death? Could a court find that it is not in my children's best interests to come and live with me?

Is it really true that my homemaker wife of thirteen years, who has stayed at home and been the primary caretaker for our children, may very well be granted physical custody, even though she stays with the paramour she left me for on the weekends I have the children? And spends time with that person and my children during the day, exposing them to the relationship? Can the court order restraints on cohabitation, and restraints on displays of affection in front of the children? If she asks the court for spousal support, will she at least have to prove by clear and convincing evidence that a denial of support would be manifestly unjust, which may be impossible to prove?

How are the state child support guidelines applied? How many of the numbers used in the calculation can we argue about? What range of numbers applies to my case? Is the range we're arguing over even that big? Would the obligation calculated under the shared custody support guidelines really be that much lower than the obligation calculated under the sole custody guidelines? Can we agree on a different number? Can child support be waived? Is that waiver enforceable? Is it a good idea to prepay my entire future child support obligation with my share of the equity in the house, or would that be a really, really bad idea?

What if my spouse and I only had a religious marriage ceremony, and never got a state civil marriage license? What if we had 500 people at our wedding, had children together, bought a house, paid taxes as a married couple and lived together for over twenty years? The court has no jurisdiction for a divorce suit, and I can't ask for property or for spousal support? Are the children illegitimate? Have we committed tax fraud? I can't get my spouse's Social Security benefits? But what if the religious marriage was performed in a country where religious-only marriages are valid?

What is a common law marriage? How is a common law marriage created? How many states recognize common law marriages? Which ones? Did we create a common law marriage by vacationing in one of those states? Does the state either one of us lives in recognize a cause of action for a palimony suit? Do any of the concepts contained in this *Guide* apply to same-sex couples with or without children?

Can I get an annulment instead of a divorce? What is the statute of limitations period pertaining to an annulment? What are the grounds for an annulment?

If I obtain, or if my spouse obtains, a religious divorce, does that mean we are legally divorced? Will the divorce court consider the religious marriage contract and the religious traditions my spouse and I are following?

Is there any such thing as a "Legal Separation," or are we simply either married or divorced? Can a suit for Separate Maintenance be filed asking for custody and support only, but not for a divorce?

It is important to hear from a locally practicing family law attorney how the courts view fault and no-fault grounds of divorce, alimony, property and debt distribution, custody, visitation and child support under your state's statutory and case law. And to then hear how the judges would view your unique situation. Then you, with your attorney, can strategize as to the best plan to attain your goals in accordance with the divorce laws of your state, and in accordance with the views of your local courts.

The internet may provide some useful information, may provide out-dated information which is not state-specific, or may provide harmfully incorrect information. Do not make major decisions without first talking with a local practicing family law attorney about likely outcomes if you were to go to court. Then let those legal factors guide you somewhat in your decision-making, and in your settlement efforts, before you wind up spending a fortune pursuing requests the judge hearing your case, and your spouse's attorney, would consider baseless.

On the other hand, even though you know your spouse is entitled to half of your thirty year pension, you don't have to just hand it to him or her on that silver platter if you know he or she isn't likely to spend the money to go to court and get it. But should you anyway? Maybe it's the right thing to do. Maybe it's also the right thing to do to pay for college for your children, even though the judge may not be able to make you.

While it is important to know the law, it may also be important to consider why the marriage broke up, the fact that you may have brought children into the world, and the reasons for the destruction of and/or reorganization of your family. It is also important to consider principles of honor, integrity, dignity, fairness and compassion.

Stop deluding yourself. Actually listen to what your spouse is saying. There may be some real validity to his or her feelings. Even if you don't believe the feelings are justified, you can't deny that your spouse actually does have those feelings. Push aside the anger and desire for revenge, push aside thoughts of vindictiveness and push aside selfishness and pettiness. Consider your spouse's and children's perspectives.

Try saying some of the following out loud:

1. If it really means that much to her, she can have it.

2. I know I don't have to pay that much child support, but I want her to be able to keep the kids involved in their activities.

3. I know my children like his new girlfriend, and she will be their stepmother. I will be happy my daughter has a step-mom at her father's house to do her hair.

4. We were married for over twenty years, and she took care of us all. I want her to be comfortable.

5. I know the baby is innocent in all this, and will be a half-brother to our children. I will welcome him into the family.

6. I know our child is better off with him, so I won't contest custody.

7. I know she and the kids will be better off if they move away, and in with her parents for a few years, while she finishes her degree.

8. I want the kids to spend as much time with their father as possible.

9. I want to give her the house. I know our children are grown, but I don't want them to hate me.

10. She's happier with him, and I wish her well.

11. He worked for it and put his life on the line, so I won't ask for any of the pension.

12. I know I don't have to agree in writing to pay for college, but I still want to.

13. Even though the court can't make me carry life insurance, I will anyway.

14. Our son will probably want to live with him in a few years. I'll let him.

15. We've agreed to name each other as trustee in our estate plans, because we trust each other, and each of us knows the kids better than anyone else.

16. I don't need a detailed visitation schedule, because we work that out just fine.

17. I'll stay on the mortgage until our youngest graduates from high school eight years from now, so you don't have to move, since I know you won't qualify to refinance.

18. We'll put into our Agreement that we will share college costs.

19. I won't ask you for any child support yet, so you'll have time to get back on your feet.

20. We'll both take the kids to the classes, practices, games, birthday parties and other activities in which they're involved. Same as when we lived together.

21. You can hold the passports.

22. How much money do you need each month?

23. How much can you pay?

24. I wouldn't want you to have to go back to work yet, so I'll pay spousal support until our youngest starts first grade.

25. What do you think is fair?

26. I know you wouldn't be able to trace your separate down payment, but I know you made it, so you can have that off the top when we sell the house.

27. We'll work out those issues regarding the kids the same way we did before the separation.

28. If you need to move down there where the cost of living isn't so high, I'll look for a place down there too, so I can stay involved in our children's lives.

29. She'll never be their mom. You are.

30. He'll never be their dad. You are.

31. I've told the children to be nice to her, and to listen to her.

32. Her fiancé can pick the children up from daycare on his way back from work, since he gets off earliest.

33. I'll pay spousal support until you finish your degree, since you left school to take care of our child.

34. I want to do what's right.

35. I want for us to remain friends when this is over.

36. I'm sorry.

The "issues" are real. The pain is real. So is the opportunity to be the best person you can, and to be the best parent you can. Say the above out loud until you no longer choke on the words. Then try saying them to your attorney, or to your spouse.

Perhaps after the Denial, Bargaining, Grief, Anger and Acceptance stages described in Chapter 1 of this *Guide*, may come the final stages of Forgiveness, Closure and Personal and/or Spiritual Growth. The experience can either beat you down, or teach you something. For those unfortunate souls who still prefer the final stage to be Revenge, at least consider that it has been said that "living well is the best revenge."

Would you act any differently if you felt your mother were watching you? Or some other person you greatly admire? What if God were actually sitting right next to you in the courtroom, seeing you testify and make your requests to the judge? If you are mediating, pull up an empty chair. If your child were sitting there watching the process, what would you be asking for, or fighting for? Are you badmouthing your spouse to your children? Using your children as messengers, or as spies? Telling them about all the court and legal proceedings? Putting your wishes before their needs? If so, stop it. Just stop.

Then do what you feel is right. Do what you can live with for the rest of your life. Do what you can be happy with when you look at yourself in the mirror every day. Do what you wouldn't mind seeing on your headstone, or in print for the public, about your actions. Do what you feel is the right thing to have done through the eyes of your children.

When you look right into their eyes, and see how you and your actions are reflected, are you pleased with yourself?

Chapter Ten

TAX CONSIDERATIONS

You don't want to run afoul of the IRS. You don't want to pay more taxes than you have to. You do want to become informed. You may want to look at IRS Publication 504 relating to *Divorced or Separated Individuals*. You may want to consult with an attorney or accountant familiar with the federal tax laws and IRS regulations.

You may want to learn more about some of the following, which are drawn from IRS publications as of the date of the publication of this *Guide*:

If you and your spouse file as married filing separate, and one of you itemizes deductions, the other of you may not be able to use the standard deduction.

You can not file as single unless you have obtained a final decree of divorce or a decree of separate maintenance by December 31st of the tax year for which you are filing.

Alimony payments are deductible from the income of the payor, who can then pay tax on less income. Alimony is includable in the income of the recipient, and therefore taxable to the recipient. Child support, however, is neither deductible from the payor's income, nor includable in the recipient's income.

For payments to be designated as alimony, they must end upon the death of the recipient, although otherwise qualifying payments could be designated as not alimony.

Payments to a third party may be alimony, such as payments for your spouse's medical expenses, rent, utilities and tuition. Life insurance premiums required to be paid on your life for a policy owned by your spouse may also be alimony. However, payments to keep up the payor's property are not alimony.

If your alimony payments terminate or decrease by a certain amount during the first three calendar years, you may be subject to the recapture rule, and you may then have to include in your income in the third year part of the alimony payments you previously deducted.

In some situations where reductions in alimony payments are clearly associated only with the happening of a contingency relating to your child, such as a child turning 18, payments you may believe are alimony may be treated by the IRS as and designated by the IRS as child support. These payments may therefore not be properly excludable from the income of the payor.

If you have been claiming a withholding exemption for your spouse, you may have to give your employer a new W-4 Form within ten days of a divorce or the signing of an Agreement, to claim your proper withholding allowances.

If you have paid alimony to your spouse, or if you have obtained a final decree of divorce or separate maintenance, you can not take an exemption for your spouse.

Although you are allowed one exemption for each person you can claim as a dependant, the exemption is phased out at higher adjusted gross incomes and may then be of no worth, unless necessary to claim head of household filing status.

Special rules determine whether a child qualifies as a dependant for which an exemption can be claimed, or can be released to a non-custodial parent. Certain "tie-breaker" rules will apply if both spouses claim the same qualifying child.

There is usually no recognized gain or loss on the transfer of property between spouses, or between former spouses, if the transfer is because of a divorce. To be incident to divorce, or related to the ending of the marriage, certain rules will apply. The transfer may have to occur within six years after the date the marriage ends. Generally the basis in property received from a spouse, or from a former spouse if incident to the divorce, will be the same as the spouse's or former spouse's adjusted basis.

The federal gift tax does not apply to most transfers of property between spouses, or between former spouses, if because of divorce. However, in some cases a gift tax return may have to be filed.

You and your spouse may each be able to exclude from capital gains taxes up to $250,000 from the sale of your main home. But if you did not own and use that property as your main home for at least two years during the five year period ending on the date of the sale, the gain may be taxable, unless your spouse or former spouse is granted use of the property under a divorce or separation instrument and uses the property as a main home.

You may be able to deduct from income the legal fees paid for tax advice in connection with a divorce, and the legal fees paid to obtain alimony, but not the legal fees and court costs to get a divorce.

If you live in one of the nine community property states, (Arizona, California, Idaho, Louisiana, Nevada, New Mexico, Texas, Washington and Wisconsin), special rules will determine your income, and how the marital community is ended.

If you obtain an annulment, you may have to file three years of amended tax returns changing your filing status to single, or if applicable, to head of household.

The provision of comprehensive tax information is beyond the scope of this book. Before you divide mutual funds without looking at the tax consequences relating to each group of stocks, before you sell off mutual funds and unintentionally incur taxable capital gains, and before you sign off on an Agreement that provides for the sale of your former marital home after more than three years from your date of separation and an "equal" division of the proceeds (without taking into account the capital gains taxes to be paid if neither of you lives in the home), find out if you and the IRS have the same view of your liability. If you don't agree with what the IRS believes is correct, and if you then get into a dispute, the IRS will usually win, one way or the other.

Chapter Eleven

CONSIDERATIONS INVOLVING MILITARY SERVICEMEMBERS

Family Support

Soldiers are required to manage their personal affairs in a manner that does not bring discredit upon themselves, or upon the military. The military takes seriously the duty of its members to provide family support. Soldiers are therefore required to conduct themselves in an honorable manner with regard to parental commitments and responsibilities. The military does not want personal problems to become an official matter of concern.

Military regulations governing the personal affairs of servicemembers set forth policy, and describe what actions can trigger a command's obligation to take action against a soldier. A mere complaint to the command, or to an authorized representative of the command, that a soldier is not providing financial support to his or her family, could trigger command action. This complaint could be by telephone call, letter, fax, email or other form of communication.

Command involvement in cases of a soldier's failure to provide financial support to family members could include the authorization of an involuntary allotment, or the ordering of a soldier to initiate a voluntary allotment. A soldier's failure to provide financial support to family members could be a violation of regulations, and punishable under the Uniform Code of Military Justice.

Take heed. Or action.

The Filing of a Case against a Servicemember

The federal Servicemembers' Civil Relief Act, or "SCRA," affords protection to servicemembers on active duty whose spouses decide to file divorce suits and conduct divorce proceedings, when servicemembers are unable to defend themselves. The SCRA applies to individuals on active duty in the military, including service in the Coast Guard, activated Reserve, activated National Guard and activated Air National Guard.

The SCRA also applies to a host of other individuals on federal active duty besides regular members of the armed forces, such as inductees serving with the armed forces, Public Health Service and National Oceanic and Atmospheric Administration Officers detailed for duty with the armed forces, persons training or studying under the supervision of the U.S. preliminary to induction, and personnel on duty for training or other duty at the request of the President for or in support of an operation during a war or declared national emergency.

If your spouse is protected under the SCRA, the divorce suit you initiate may be stayed under the Act. If it is not, you may have to pay for a lawyer for your servicemember spouse, unless he or she hires his or her own lawyer, or signs a Military Waiver waiving the rights provided by the Act.

A number of states have also enacted a patchwork of statutes attempting to protect the parental rights of deployed servicemembers to the permanent custody of their children. Until a uniform law in this area is enacted, certain states will continue to have varying protections and requirements addressing the needs of deploying and returning servicemembers. You will need to see what procedures apply in your jurisdiction, if you are involved in custody proceedings.

Military Benefits

There are many ins and outs regarding spousal entitlement to military benefits. You should obtain answers to those of the below questions relevant to your, or to your spouse's, military service.

Who handles continued healthcare benefits for a qualified former spouse? What is the Defense Eligibility Enrollment Reporting System (DEERS) Office?

Were contributions made by the servicemember to the Uniformed Services Thrift Savings Plan, or military TSP? Would the nonmember be entitled to a portion of those benefits? What sort of court order would have to be prepared to transfer any of those benefits?

Must 10 years of my marriage overlap with 10 years earned by my spouse of military service creditable for retired pay, in order for me to receive direct payment of my share of my spouse's military retirement from the Defense Finance and Accounting Service, or "DFAS?" Am I eligible for a renewable military identification card, and for limited health benefits, if 15 years of the marriage overlapped with military service? Full medical, post exchange, commissary and theater privileges with 20 years if I remain unmarried?

What happens if disposable retired pay is waived by my spouse in order to receive disability payments – whether Concurrent Retirement and Disability Payments (CRDP) or Concurrent Disability Payments (CDP)? If DFAS will not pay me, a former spouse, any portion of Concurrent Disability Payments received by my spouse, a servicemember, will my share of the disposable retired pay be reduced? Can language be drafted for a court order, or for an Agreement, that will protect me if my spouse converts his or her retirement pay to disability pay?

If my spouse elects to receive a Career Status Bonus, will that reduce the monthly retirement benefit? Can I receive a portion of the bonus from DFAS?

If the benefits are important to me, the spouse of the military member, should I work with a professional familiar with all the ins and outs under military benefits law? Can my spouse and I mutually agree to delay the date of retirement from the military, or delay the date of our final separation, or delay the date of submission of our final divorce decree for entry by the judge, until we hit either 5, 10, 15 or 20 years of marriage overlapping with creditable years of military service earned?

If I want to receive survivor benefits, must the benefits be elected before my spouse retires? Must the election be set forth in a certified copy of a final divorce decree sent to DFAS in Kentucky within one year of entry, along with a Deemed Election Letter signed by me and the applicable DD form? If that is not done, would that election stop for good, even if I had been elected in the past? If I want to receive my share of the disposable retired pay, must certified copies of a final divorce decree and of a Qualifying Court Order be sent to DFAS in Ohio, along with the applicable DD form? Will I lose survivor benefits if I remarry before age 55?

Am I still eligible for military medical care if I, an unremarried former spouse, am also covered by an employer-sponsored health plan? Can the military health coverage be reinstated if I lose that private coverage? Are the benefits unable to be reinstated, and lost for good, if I remarry and then divorce, or if my new spouse dies? Does it make any difference if I was at least 55 years old when I remarried? Are private supplemental health insurance plans also available through the military? For how many years after the divorce can the spouse of the member remain eligible for that coverage?

Can life insurance coverage be maintained on my life, the spouse of the enlisted military member, under Servicemembers' Group Life Insurance, (SGLI), or Veteran's Group Life Insurance, (VGLI), for a retired member? Will this be discontinued if we divorce?

If my spouse receives survivor benefits as a result of my military service, does that reduce the amount of retired pay I will receive? If I do not want my spouse to receive those survivor benefits, can I prevent my spouse forever from being awarded survivor benefits in the future if I retire and don't make the election? If I have already retired, and I elected for my spouse to receive the survivor benefit, I can never remove that election? If I am not yet retired, and we are not yet divorced, would my spouse be required to sign a Waiver of those rights if I do not want to elect survivor benefits for my spouse, or if I want to choose limited benefits?

If the divorce decree doesn't mention survivor benefits, or if it does but a certified copy is not sent to DFAS within one year, is my spouse's right to the benefit lost for good, even if I am already retired and my spouse had been previously designated? But could my estate be forced to pay the value of the benefit upon my death if DFAS doesn't?

Can I choose deferred benefits to be received by my spouse either immediately after I, the member, die before age 60, or only to be received by my spouse after I *would have* reached 60 years of age if I die before I reach age 60? If I served in the Reserves, can survivor benefits be received by my spouse after I have 20 good years of service, up until I die or would have turned 60 if I die sooner? If I elect the Reserve Component Survivor Benefit Plan to cover those intervening years, will there be an actuarial reduction in the benefits paid later? Are the rules any different for the National Guard?

Do you, the servicemember, feel your spouse should receive none of your military retirement, because you were the one who put your life on the line, and earned it? Do you, the military spouse, feel you earned that pension just as much as your spouse by relocating many times, with all the attendant packing, unpacking, and searching for new doctors and dentists; by putting your career on hold, or continually starting and stopping your career with each move; by being a supportive military spouse, scared to death each time the doorbell rang at odd hours while your spouse was deployed; by trying to help your spouse readjust to civilian life after deployment; and by having possibly borne the brunt of the nonadjustment after return which contributed to the ending of the marriage?

If you don't know which of the above questions pertain to your situation, and the answers to those questions that do pertain, you need the assistance of a military retirement benefits specialist.

Chapter Twelve

WHAT ABOUT THE CHILDREN?

Should we tell our children?

Imagine that many of your coworkers are getting laid off from work, and you know that more layoffs are coming. Imagine that every few months, with each round of cuts moving closer and closer, you watch another friend and member of your department sadly empty out his or her desk. The fear and uncertainty of your waiting to be axed can be worse than the knowing, and the stress of waiting for the other shoe to fall can be excruciating. But when you know that something is definite, you can step up to the plate, show your strength of character and what you are made of, and can get informed, make plans and take action.

Newsflash: Your kids know something is up, and that mom and dad aren't getting along. It is not usually normal for mom and dad to never sleep together, especially if they don't ever show affection to each other, or for mom to be crying all the time, or to see increasingly acrimonious fights. Your children have friends whose parents put their kids through horrible divorces. Your children's imaginations can create scenarios far worse than reality. They fear that they may never see one of you anymore, that one of you won't be there for them anymore, that they are not loved anymore, that your fighting is all their fault and that Santa may not come on Christmas Day.

Alleviate the tension and anxiety by coming out and letting your children know you will be forming a two-home family, and that they will become two-home children.

How and what should we tell our children?

Tell them together. Keep it simple and brief. Leave the adult issues out of it. Would you let your children watch an X-rated movie? Give them the G-rated version of events. That's all they need.

Tell them the decision to separate and divorce is mutual. Tell your children it is not the fault of one or the other of you, that you and your spouse simply cannot continue to live together, and that they are not to blame. It is important for your children to understand that your separation and divorce is not their fault.

Tell them they will have two homes, and that they will still see each of you. Tell them you will do some things all together as a family on occasion, but that does not mean you and your spouse will be getting back together. Tell them you love them very much, that you will always love them very much and that nothing could *ever* change that. Tell them you will both be at their games and school events, and will cooperate in taking them to those events, regardless of which home they will be at on that day.

When should we tell our children?

Don't wait until the boxes are piled up in the hallway. On the other hand, don't tell them if nothing is going to happen for awhile. Tell them sometime in between – when something is set to change in the near future. Give them time to process the change before it's a done deal. If they're watching you check out schools, daycare centers and apartments in a new town, you've waited too long.

What should we *not* tell our children?

Don't tell them how stressed, sad, hurt, scared and angry you are. It is *not* a child's job to absorb an adult's pain and frustration. Don't tell them how bad a person or parent your spouse is. It *is* a child's job to love each parent, warts and all. Don't tell them all about how evil your spouse's paramour is.

Don't tell them you can't afford your home any more because of your spouse. Don't tell them you are worried about having enough money.

Don't tell them that your spouse doesn't love them or want to see them anymore. Don't tell them your spouse is a threat to them unless that is *absolutely* true, and you obtain counseling for them to process that truth. Don't tell them about judges, lawyers and court proceedings. It's your job as a parent to insulate them from the negativity your divorce is creating, and to help them cope with the fallout of the restructuring of the family. They won't read self-help books. You can, and should.

Will news of the impending separation and divorce affect our children of different ages in different ways?

Yes. Very young children may simply need to know that there is a plan, and that everything will be all right. They don't necessarily need to know all the details of who's going to refinance the former marital home, or what the custodial schedule will look like. The average four year old doesn't even *know* what a "weekend" *is*, let alone the concept of alternate weekends. Small children just need to know that they'll still see mom and dad all the time. Each morning they may only need to know what they'll be doing that day, and when they go to bed, after talking at least on the phone with their other parent to say goodnight, what they'll be doing after they wake up.

Older children will want reassurance that their lives will not be disrupted too much, and that their needs will be taken care of. They may insist that nothing in their lives should change. That may not, however, be entirely possible.

If you *are* going to disrupt your children's lives by moving them out of their schools or away from their friends, show them how to properly bereave in going through the process of loss. Be an example to them of how to look forward with optimism, because curveballs and change are a part of life. Make them understand that if they have to move into a smaller home, the brick and mortar do not define their self worth.

Teach them gently that it is important for them to learn how to move through the hard changes. They don't have to "keep a stiff upper lip." It is healthy and necessary for them to feel an appropriate level of pain. Just as you must, your children must experience and move through that pain. If they just suppress or repress their anxiety and fear, they will simply develop more and greater problems later on.

What actions are the most hurtful to our children?

Judges, divorce lawyers, and family therapists see the fallout when one parent acts in ways that are harmful to children. Parents who intentionally or unintentionally harm their children often do so because of significant untreated mental health or substance abuse issues. A parent may also be unable to cope because he or she is overwhelmed with the burdens of caring for children, while also working outside the home, with minimal or no help. Cultural issues may leave a parent feeling trapped in an unhealthy marriage, or unable to stand up for himself or herself and the children during a separation. A parent may be codependent upon, or the victim of, an abusive spouse, and not yet emotionally healthy or strong enough to leave his or her abuser.

A parent may also suffer from milder mental health problems, such as not being able to control his or her anger towards an unfaithful spouse. A parent unable to deal with the offending spouse in a healthy manner may act in ways that seem erratic, excessively selfish or downright mean. The family may also not even realize a parent has a problem such as depression, bipolar disorder or borderline personality disorder, which problems can cause that person to act in harmful or overly controlling ways.

Parents caught up in their own dramas need to understand and take the following to heart:

Children can become emotionally damaged by watching a parent spend a lot of time crying on the phone to friends and family, or by watching him or her engage in unnecessary theatrics. Children can become emotionally damaged when a parent's new social life impacts their care.

Children can become emotionally damaged by watching one parent damage their other parent's property out of anger or spite. Children can become emotionally damaged when one parent badmouths their other parent, and their other parent's paramour, to them and to everyone else.

Children can become emotionally damaged if they are constantly hearing one parent complain that their other parent is not sending enough money. Children can become emotionally damaged when they see a parent keep track of how much money is spent on them when they are with that parent, as if that parent is deciding just how much they are worth.

Children can become emotionally damaged if they are told to act as spies, and to report on their other parent's actions. Children can become emotionally damaged if they are asked to relay messages back and forth about support and visitation.

Children can become emotionally damaged when one parent tries to cut their other parent out of their lives, when that parent poses no threat to them. Children can become emotionally damaged when one parent won't let them talk, unmonitored and frequently, to their other parent on the telephone.

Children can become emotionally damaged when one parent calls the police all the time when their non-violent, non-threatening other parent merely comes by the school, extracurricular activities or former marital home to see them. Children can become emotionally damaged when they see one parent bar their other parent from the former marital home just after the initial separation, without good cause.

Children can become emotionally damaged when a parent *should* call the police because they are being physically abused, and does not. Children can become emotionally damaged when a parent tells a child to lie to the school or doctor or else the *children* will be "putting mommy or daddy in jail," instead of clarifying that mommy or daddy put his or her *own* self into jail for improper conduct.

Children can become emotionally damaged when a parent tolerates their other parent's emotional abuse of them, and remains silent. Children can become emotionally damaged when a parent accepts abuse as a matter of course, thereby teaching his or her children that it is acceptable to live with abuse.

Children can become emotionally damaged when their parents jockey to get to the school or daycare center first to pick them up, just so their other parent can't. Children can become emotionally damaged when their parents fight over enrolling them in August in different school districts, because their parents think they're fighting over some perceived advantage in the custody hearing they want to have.

Children can become emotionally damaged when a parent moves out, and they do not see that parent's new place, no matter how humble. They need to know where that parent is, and that he or she is all right. Children can become emotionally damaged when they need to spend extra time with the parent who just moved out to be reassured that parent is still there for them, and the other parent won't let them, out of fear of setting a custodial timesharing precedent.

Children can become emotionally damaged when they are forced to spend time with a parent's new love interest, when they are not ready to have that person in their lives, or don't like that person. Children can become emotionally damaged when they see their parent prefer to spend time with that new interest instead of with them, or if that person takes time away from their time with their parent.

Children can become emotionally damaged when a parent moves away with them, far from the other parent, and they no longer see the other parent on a regular basis. Children can become emotionally damaged when a parent moves away from them, making them feel rejected and abandoned. They will always be missing someone.

Children can become emotionally damaged when a parent tries to tell them what they should "tell the judge" at the upcoming custody hearing. Children can become emotionally damaged when their parents tell them all about and involve them in court proceedings. Children can become emotionally damaged when their parents try to get them to choose between them.

Children can become emotionally damaged when a parent constantly promises to pick them up on a certain day at a certain time, and doesn't show up or is always late. Children can become emotionally damaged when their parents fight during and about each visitation exchange.

Children can become emotionally damaged when conflict swirls around special holidays and birthdays. Children can become emotionally damaged when their parents cause public scenes at their sporting, school and other special events.

Children can become emotionally damaged when a parent won't take them to the activities they want to participate in, because the other parent set up the activities. Children can become emotionally damaged when a parent won't let them take the clothing or toys purchased for them to their other parent's home so they can have them there also.

Children can become emotionally damaged when you try to sling mud at each other in a custody case, hoping some of it will stick. The reality is that judges want to hear the positive of what you can each offer your children, and not the negatives. That mud usually winds up splashing right back onto the person who threw it.

Children can become emotionally damaged when they see you hurt each other.

Children caught in the crossfire may become traumatized, and may be reduced to little puddles of anxiety. Or they may not always show on the outside just how much damage you are doing to them - at least maybe not right away. They may even deny to themselves the pain they are feeling. That suppressed pain, fear and anger will remain with them, however, and will affect them down the road.

Children who do not receive the appropriate help to process what they are being put through will act out their stresses later on in ways destructive to themselves, to their futures, to their adult relationships and to society. That will be the legacy of your divorce.

Is it sometimes necessary to protect children from a parent?

It is wrong to alienate children from a parent unless that parent is abusive *to the children* and is not addressing that problem. If a parent is abusive *to the other parent*, the victim must learn, through therapy, to set appropriate limits and boundaries with the abuser, and must teach the children to set those same limits. However, if the limits are conveyed to the abuser and are then crossed, it may become appropriate at that time in some cases to redefine the relationship.

If a parent is suffering from a significant untreated mental health problem, his or her children of any age could benefit from therapy to learn to understand that problem. They will need to learn to set appropriate limits to avoid being victimized, and to allay their fears that they will suffer the same fate someday. It may be necessary, in extreme cases, to set limits through protective court orders requiring restrictions on visitation, or by requiring visitation to be supervised.

If a parent is suffering from a significant untreated substance abuse problem, his or her children should also receive professional help, so they can avoid becoming sympathetic enablers, especially if that was the behavior modeled by their other parent. It would also be advisable to become familiar with the documented problems faced by children of substance abusers, (including untreated "dry drunks" who are still alcoholics even though not drinking), so as to learn to spot and help those children overcome the other negative coping behaviors they may develop.

Children of substance abusers may have to grow up just a bit faster than children not exposed to such problems, so they can learn how to spot signs of a parent's substance abuse when in that parent's care. They should be given and learn to use a cell phone, so they can call for help if their safety is put in jeopardy. Voluntary or court-ordered restrictions on visitation, or supervised visitation, may also be appropriate.

If your spouse is engaging in any of the above behaviors, you must find the financial resources and time to take whatever action is necessary to save your children. If you don't help them, you may be just as guilty of abusing them as is your spouse. Don't teach them to accept and live with unacceptable behavior.

And if *you* are engaging in these behaviors yourself, you must get professional help so you can cope, get on track and not ruin your children's futures even further.

How can we help our children?

Be there for them. Let them cry. Don't relax all oversight in a misguided guilt-driven belief that they can't maintain their normal responsibilities, but cut them some slack once in a while.

Have them attend at least one or two sessions with a competent mental health practitioner specializing in family counseling and the treatment of children. Keep them in counseling if necessary. Let the school guidance counselor know what's going on. See if the school has a support group for kids whose parents are divorcing.

Do something special for them every now and then. Spend time with them. Let them have some fun. Have some fun with them. Laugh once in awhile.

Most importantly, never let them see, hear or know about you fighting with your spouse. Don't create a tempest and expect your children to just calmly sail through it.

Work out your differences outside of court.

Chapter Thirteen

WHAT IS A SETTLEMENT AGREEMENT?

So, you've both decided to settle, instead of going to court. Good for you. Now you "just need to put it in writing." Maybe you have some of the questions set forth below.

If we settle everything without going to court, is a document drawn up and sent to a judge?

Yes.

An attorney or an attorney mediator will draw up an Agreement, either before, during or after litigation has commenced. An Agreement may be prepared by an attorney mediator, by a collaborative attorney or by an attorney hired for negotiation or for litigation. The Agreement becomes a binding contract when signed. If either you or your spouse violates the Agreement, you could be sued for breach of contract. The document will be submitted into evidence during the court case, and will be incorporated into your final divorce decree. It will then also become a binding court order. If either one of you violates the terms of the Agreement later on, you could be held in contempt of a court order.

The Agreement is actually a settlement of a case either of you could bring for property division, debt division, alimony, custody, visitation and/or child support. Viewed in that light, it is important to understand that you can't make your spouse sign an Agreement. You can't make your spouse settle his or her case. If you do not reach an agreement, if you do not want to give in to your spouse on everything, and if you do not want to maintain the in-limbo *status quo,* you will have to go to court, put on your case and ask the judge to enter an order granting your requests.

Reaching an agreement outside of court is very often the preferable way to go.

If we do an Agreement, do we have to agree to what the law would require of us if we went to court?

No.

If you work out an agreement, there are no rules. Anything goes as long as it is legal. You do not have to do what the judge would do if he or she heard your case. You are free to craft solutions a judge wouldn't think of, wouldn't order or wouldn't take the time to put together.

You should, however, enter into your Agreement with a full understanding of what would likely happen if you went to court, in order to evaluate the reasonableness of your positions. If you agree to provisions such as a waiver of child support, you need to understand that some provisions, and you need to understand which ones, if any, may not be enforceable, or may have no teeth as drafted.

Do we need to sign and put an Agreement in place before we separate?

No.

You can reach agreement, and sign a document embodying those agreements, either before you separate, or after. You may settle before a case is filed, or after. You may settle on the eve of trial, or on the day of trial. Sooner is usually preferable to later, if the goal is to avoid unnecessary turmoil and attorney's fees. Exactly when an Agreement is prepared and presented to you, or to your spouse, is a matter of mutual planning or of separate strategy.

What is the Agreement called?

The document may have any of a number of titles such as: Separation Agreement; Separation and Property Settlement Agreement; Custody, Support and Property Agreement; Mediated Separation Agreement; Collaborative Settlement Agreement; or very commonly, Property Settlement Agreement or "PSA." Attorneys often talk of "PSAs." What you call the document doesn't matter.

Do I need a lawyer to prepare the Agreement?

Yes.

Yes.

Yes.

You need a lawyer to prepare your Agreement.

You need a lawyer to prepare your Agreement.

You need a lawyer to prepare your Agreement.

And if your spouse's attorney has prepared the Agreement, you need your own lawyer to review that Agreement for you, and to inform you of all the important little omissions and phrases which will certainly need to be added, deleted or corrected in order to protect you. Phrases such as "exclusive possession," "timely indemnify and hold harmless" and "relinquish and waive all future claims." These little words actually do have very important meaning. You are not a lawyer. You will not even realize there were problems, or know what words should have been included to protect your interests but weren't, no matter how smart you are. The smart thing to do is to pay someone in the beginning, to make sure you don't pay even more in the end.

If I don't like the Agreement my spouse has given me, what should I do?

Don't sign it. It's just a proposal – a starting point in the negotiation.

If a letter accompanying the Agreement "only gives you" some amount of time "to respond," you still don't have to do anything. You can throw the proposal right in the trash if you want to. No one can make you settle until you are ready.

But there is such a thing as waiting too long.

If you won't negotiate or sign anything, because you want to keep milking your spouse's generosity for as long as possible, you will find that that generosity will lessen as your spouse's frustration with you grows, and may ultimately end completely. Animosity will increase between you, harming the children, because of your unwillingness to move forward. If you refuse to address the situation in a timely manner, you will wind up years behind the curve in your efforts to get your life back, and in your efforts to reestablish yourself in the job market, with only yourself to blame.

Don't wait so long to resolve matters that you hurt yourself in the long run, and are forced to settle for a less desirable result, and at greater cost.

If you are going to have to support yourself in the future, start getting yourself ready to get back into the workforce Right Now, especially if you are a female in your late forties. Don't put all your eggs in one basket, unless you are holding the basket.

Get an attorney to review the Agreement. See how far apart you are. File a lawsuit if your views are so far apart they can't be settled, before your spouse does and you lose all control over your life. Or you may wish to discuss mediating the differences you each have with the proposal. Or you may discuss whether you could resolve your disagreements collaboratively. Or if you hire an attorney, you and your attorney could negotiate the Agreement adversarially with your spouse's attorney.

If I like the Agreement my spouse has given me, should I just sign?

Absolutely not. If you are ready to move forward with a settlement, if your spouse's attorney has prepared the first draft, it is vital that you not sign the Agreement unless you at least have the Agreement reviewed by an attorney who has only your interests in mind. No matter how much pressure is put on you to sign. No matter how much you want to "keep it simple" without "getting all the lawyers involved." No matter how conflict averse you are. To request revisions so the Agreement clearly and appropriately reflects what you and your spouse may have verbally agreed upon, or to request revisions that are fair to you, should not create conflict.

You have to involve a lawyer to review the Agreement for you. Your spouse's attorney does not care what you want, does not represent you and may even mislead you. You should not trust that attorney no matter how nice, how sympathetic or how agreeable he or she might seem. That attorney will have properly done his or her job to draft an Agreement that protects only his or her client, and not you. Sure you may want to "get it all over with" real bad. But if you don't do it right, you may find that the problems are not really over just by your signing off on your spouse's proposal, and will blow up with a vengeance in the future, right in your face.

If we can agree on everything, can my spouse and I just write up an Agreement on our own, maybe using a copy of a friend's Agreement, or one we get off the internet, to save money?

Only if your divorce does not involve spousal support, retirement, significant assets or a house, and even then for you to write up an Agreement yourselves would probably still be a bad idea. Most likely, the document will not be specific as to your state's laws, and will not be tailored to your situation and life. Later on, when you and your spouse may not be on such friendly terms, especially if you have no minor children keeping you involved with each other, you will realize that the document did not protect you. You will then spend more money on attorneys, trying to fix, trying to clarify and unsuccessfully trying to undo what should have been done properly in the first place, and then you will pay a higher price.

If my spouse and I have agreed on everything, why don't we just decide which of us will hire an attorney to draw up an Agreement, and the other of us will just sign that Agreement?

You could. But if you just sign off on the Agreement your spouse tosses at you, you will have taken small part in creating your future. The Agreement will be drafted from your spouse's perspective, and will contain subtle biases and omissions which are not in your favor. If instead you hire the attorney to draw up the Agreement, and the Agreement is mailed to your spouse, or left on the kitchen table, your spouse may feel left out of the process, and as if he or she is simply signing off on your requests without any involvement or input in the decision-making.

The Agreement will contain lots of language like "whereas," "hereby" and "aforementioned," and will refer to your family as "the parties" and "said children." The home you may remain in with the children will be termed "the former marital residence."

You could instead participate jointly and equally in the process redefining your family and your life, and could create your futures together. By using collaboration or mediation, you can have an Agreement prepared which is written more simply, which refers to all of the members of your family by name, and which does not contain a lot of stuffy, old-fashioned and unnecessary legal jargon.

Should the Agreement cover every detail and possibility that could occur?

It can't. You have to draw the line somewhere. If you each want a high level of control and predictability, you may try to define what the plan will be in each and every contingency, but you won't be able to cover every possible event that could occur.

If you and your spouse have a high level of trust in each other, certain provisions within your Agreement may be very general, rather vague or even aspirational. You may state that visitation with the children, extracurricular activities and the costs for college shall be "as mutually agreed upon." On the other hand, if you lack trust in each other, you may set forth a detailed visitation plan that defines who gets the kids on which holidays in even and odd years, starting with which one of you in which year, from what time to what time, and where the visitation exchange will take place. You may merely state that you will divide your household goods by agreement, or you may feel the need to attach two comprehensive lists of possessions as an Attachment to your document. It may be very important to you to clarify for the record just who gets the shower curtains. Or not.

You, your spouse and your attorney should know and define just how much protection is necessary or desirable based upon the assets involved, your unique relationship, your family history, your children's needs and the current situation.

What is the actual purpose of the Agreement?

Most lawyers will tell you that the purpose of writing agreements down in a contract, and then having the contract signed, is so you can sue the other party in court if he or she violates any of the contract's provisions. Viewed in this way, the purpose of the Agreement is to create a binding, enforceable document which the other party must obey, and if he or she doesn't, the court will make him or her do what was promised.

You may decide, however, to include aspirational provisions in your Agreement. These provisions merely indicate that you've considered a particular matter, such as college costs for a child or extracurricular activity costs, but can only promise to contribute financially "to the extent you are able" or "only if the choice of activities is mutually agreed upon." You may agree to waive child support. Provisions drafted in a certain way may not protect either one of you, and may not be enforceable. Aspirational provisions may, however, indicate that you jointly considered certain matters, and that you have a certain intent, which intent may or may not ever be realized. Or you may each in good faith do your best to attain your aspirational goals, and will succeed in making them a reality.

What if we jointly decide not to follow the Agreement we signed?

You can.

The world won't stop spinning, and you won't be arrested. The terms of your Agreement, in some sense, such as those provisions pertaining to a visitation schedule, can be viewed as a sort of fallback if you don't agree otherwise. You're not breaking the law if you begin to follow a different visitation schedule by mutual agreement.

But be very clear. If you decide to do *anything* other than what you agreed in writing to do, and then have a falling out with your ex-spouse, perhaps when one of you starts dating another, you each have the right to enforce the terms of the original written Agreement. This is true regardless of the fact that you have both been doing otherwise, regardless of for how long you have been doing otherwise, and regardless of your verbal agreement to do otherwise. Possibly even regardless of the contract you both signed modifying your original Agreement, but which contract you didn't incorporate into a new court order to modify the order which incorporated your original Agreement. And even if you don't mind the lower amount paid for the buyout of your equity in the home, if you die perhaps your executor or heirs will, and they may have standing to file a lawsuit, using assets from your estate to pay the legal fees to sue your ex-spouse.

If you verbally agree to a higher or lower support amount, or home equity buyout, than what your Agreement states, rock beats scissors, and paper beats air.

Can we modify our Agreement in the future, or are we stuck with it forever?

Yes and yes.

Provisions regarding property, debt and almost all other matters are usually considered to be carved in stone. That means that if one of you changes your mind, and the other doesn't, the Agreement will not be changed. But if you both agree, you can always do an Addendum, or a Modification Agreement, to be incorporated into a new court order, changing anything from the first Agreement.

However, understand that if you don't incorporate a Modification Agreement into a new court order, the Modification Agreement may not be enforceable. Rock beats scissors, and orders beat agreements.

Some provisions, such as those involving child support, custody and visitation, will always be modifiable if a significant change in circumstances occurs after entry of a previous court order, such as the original order incorporating your Agreement. That means you can always go to court later on and try to change those provisions.

Spousal support provisions may or may not be modifiable, depending upon the wording of the document. That wording is therefore critical. Make sure you are very clear as to whether any spousal support payments will either be modifiable, or nonmodifiable, in your Agreement.

But don't bank on making future revisions when you sign your original document, regardless of what your spouse may be telling you about "just separating to work on the marriage," and even if you're still in denial and think you'll eventually get back together. Before you sign your name to any Agreement, be sure you can live with what that document states, forever.

Will the Agreement be a public record?

Usually, yes. Our court system is supposed to be open, so your document will be placed in a court file folder with your name on it, and the folder will be kept somewhere in the courthouse before it may be moved to Archives, or scanned and destroyed. Your file may even be recorded in public computer records.

Will anyone care to read your divorce papers over at the courthouse? Probably not. Maybe. Is there anything you can do to prevent your life from being available for anyone to peruse? Probably not. Maybe.

Some courts will at least have a separate filing system not available to the public, and not put into the public computer records, for private matters such as social security numbers, and asset and debt account numbers. But the details of the boozing, infidelity, cruelty or visitation arrangements involving your family are not considered private. You may ask your attorney to seek a protective order sealing your case from the public eyes, but in the absence of good cause, the court will assume that inquiring minds have a right to know.

Chapter Fourteen

WHAT HAPPENS IF WE GO TO COURT?

Sometimes you need to stop being so nice. If your generosity is not appreciated or reciprocated and you're the only one giving in, you may simply be letting yourself be taken advantage of. Mediation, collaboration and negotiation are not options if your spouse's participation would only be in bad faith. If your case just won't settle, despite all your best efforts, and if there are reasons to go forward with litigation, off you will go. As you journey down that path, you may want to know what "going to court" will entail, which is described for you below.

As you will see, litigation involves a tremendous amount of time, effort and cost. Don't litigate if you can't commit to that time, effort and cost, or you will lose. You need to be very involved in the process, you will have a lot of work to do, and you will have many meetings and hearings to attend. You can't just leave it all with your lawyer.

If you are employed, you will miss hours and days of work. If you are a clear thinker, and are good with the computer, your attorney should let you do as much analysis and document reviews as you are able. For every hour or so you spend doing summaries of documents, or preparing exhibits for your attorney, you can pay that much less to your attorney. Your attorney, however, can't just leave it all with you either. Be sure you are comfortable working closely with your lawyer.

You and your lawyer will work together very hard to get ready for THE BIG DAY. Below are set forth the steps you will take to get there.

1. **Filing and Service of the Case**

First, a case must be filed with the court alleging fault or no-fault divorce grounds. The papers will ask for a divorce, and for any other relief you may seek, such as spousal support, property and debt division, a restraint on the dissipation of assets, custody, visitation, child support and for an award of attorney's fees. There may also be a request for a restraining order, or for exclusive possession of the former marital home. Usually everything is thrown in there by the lawyer "just in case." The case may allege fault grounds which an attorney somewhat inflated, so as to be able to file suit without having to wait a year, planning to amend the grounds later on to no-fault grounds, or the suit may be a simple request for a divorce based on living separate and apart for the requisite time period.

The case has to be served. You may come home one day to see that the Sheriff has taped a bright yellow plastic bag containing papers to your front door, serving you by posting. Or, for impact, you may be personally served by private process server at work, at a party or at some other embarrassing locale. Perhaps service of a one-half inch thick lawsuit will be made upon you at the office Christmas party, at the club on your birthday, or at home on Valentine's Day. You may never have realized your spouse could be so creative and thoughtful.

You may be served with only the initial document, or with lots of additional documents, such as discovery requests, a Motion for Temporary Relief, and a Notice of the date on which that initial Motion will be heard in court. The papers may include a Notice of Deposition for you to appear in your spouse's attorney's office, along with your paramour, to be deposed under oath before a certified court reporter. The more stuff you're served with, the more money you will be charged when you go to hire an attorney. Your spouse's lawyer knows that. You know that your spouse, in a very real sense, wants to make you pay.

There will be deadlines by which you will be told you have to respond to the suit, or else you will have to get leave of court to file late pleadings, and you will be all worried about these deadlines. Some deadlines, however, can usually be extended. But be very careful about the deadline for responding to any Requests for Admissions. If you miss that deadline, and if your spouse's attorney won't grant you an extension, your case may be weakened considerably.

2. **Discovery**

At the beginning of the case, each side will conduct discovery, so as to "discover" all the facts of the case. You may have to answer thirty written Interrogatories under oath, and will have to send those written answers to your spouse's attorney within 21 or 28 days of when served upon you. You may receive Requests to either admit or deny various statements, also under oath.

There will be a Request for Production of Documents. You will have to produce those documents by the deadline for receipt, or face a Motion to Compel Production. Requests for documents such as pay-stubs, tax returns, retirement statements, account information, mortgage information, your credit card receipts and statements, copies of your check registers and bank statements, notebooks and diaries, and maybe even a copy of your computer hard drive may all be permissible, standard requests.

If you think you can get out of producing all of that, think again. If you don't answer and turn over what was asked for, a Motion to Compel may be filed, and the court will make you respond. You may then even have to pay your spouse's attorney's fees for their having to compel you to comply with their requests. If you don't have the requested information anymore, you may be ordered to go and get it.

If you say you just don't have and therefore can't produce requested information, (really because you're hoping to hide that information), or if you try to misstate information, understand that verifiable documentation can usually be obtained by your spouse elsewhere. Subpoenas for documents may be sent to instate entities such as banks and financial institutions, to your current and former employers and to the credit card companies, seeking copies of all of your files. In some cases, requests for documents can also be sent out of state. Computer server records and telephone records may perhaps be obtained.

Notices of Depositions may be filed with the court, and served upon you. Subpoenas may be issued summoning your friends, family, paramour, paramour's spouse, coworkers, neighbors and acquaintances to your spouse's attorney's office, to answer questions under oath before a court reporter. Those people may then feel the need to hire attorneys on each of their own individual behalf. Your paramour may be worried about incriminating himself or herself if adultery is still on the books as a state crime. He or she may be worried about any impact on his or her security clearances, or public reputation.

Your final trial date may be set early on in the case, or may be set later on. That final hearing date will probably be six, eight or ten months from the date the case is filed, when the court has an unscheduled day or two free on the docket, and by when your attorneys feel they will be ready for trial. The date also has to be set for when neither attorney has any conflicts with hearing dates in other cases, and not set too close to their scheduled vacations.

Prior to that, you may have a short (less than one-half day) hearing on a Motion for Temporary Relief, seeking entry of a Temporary Order granting either of you temporary custody, visitation, child support, spousal support or a restraint to keep things calm until THE BIG DAY. You may also have other hearings on other motions prior to trial. You may have one final all-day custody hearing, at some point between the initial filing of the case, and the date of the final hearing.

Perhaps you forget what is in the house you vacated over a year ago, and you therefore want to inventory and videotape the interior and the contents of the house. Then you can figure out what to ask the judge to make your spouse give back to you at the final hearing. How long you can stay in the house during such an inventory, whether you can open drawers and closets, and whom you and your spouse may have present as witnesses during the inventory, will all have to be negotiated or litigated. Perhaps someone is violating the Temporary Order. Your attorneys will find lots of things to call to the court's attention prior to the final hearing.

Although your trial date is six months or more away, you and your attorneys will all hardly have enough time to do discovery, analyze all the documents and deposition transcripts, line up expert witnesses, get property appraised, do a business valuation if applicable and analyze all the numbers regarding separate and marital shares of all the finances. You will all be very busy.

3. Experts

You, and those like you, mere "lay" witnesses, can only testify in court as to facts. Only "expert" witnesses can render opinions. You are certainly not qualified in the eyes of the law to give opinion testimony as to anything. Although on a philosophical level it could be argued whether the statement, "The sky is blue" is fact or opinion, the lawyers and the judge will usually have similar ideas as to which matters you can talk about, and which matters will require expert testimony.

If you want to value a house, a business or certain other assets, or if you want to talk about someone's mental or physical health, point out that someone could be earning more money, or testify that for mental health reasons the children should live with you and not with your spouse, you will usually have to hire someone to come to court and say what you want him or her to say. Of course the learned expert is objective, and there is only one true answer. But if both you and your spouse's experts had reached the same conclusions, you wouldn't be paying them each to come to court, now would you?

4. Pretrial Matters

Your local court may set a Pretrial Conference, during which you all inform the court of which matters will be heard at trial on THE BIG DAY. The judge may want to know how long your case will take, in order to have a firm idea as to when to schedule a tee time on that day. Or the judge would like an idea as to how long he or she will be on the bench that day, so as to determine when he or she can get back to Chambers and do some of the other work piled up on the desk, or to know whether he or she can make the committed-to public service event which is scheduled for early evening on the day of your trial.

Counsel may enter into a few stipulations, or agreements, as to some values or issues. Various motions regarding evidence may be argued and ruled on at various times prior to THE BIG DAY. The court may order you to attend a Settlement Conference with a retired judge, to try to get you to work out your differences. You may both be required to attend a parenting class. In some jurisdictions, the judges will try to put as many requirements and hoops to jump through as they can, between the filing of your case and the final hearing date, to try to get you to settle, to streamline the process and to eliminate surprise.

There will be a date by which you must each identify all of your witnesses, disclose what your experts will say and identify every document you intend to introduce into evidence at trial. There will be another date by which you must object to any evidence the other side proposes to submit, that you feel they should not be entitled to submit. If you miss that date, you may have missed your right to object at trial. An inadvertent waiver of that right could be very damaging, if not fatal, to your case.

5. **Preparation of Testimony**

All of the witnesses must be prepared. That means the testimony should be discussed and rehearsed. Your witnesses should know what they will be asked. You need to know what they will say. You don't want to contradict them. They must be educated as to the avoidance of hearsay evidence. Your attorney wants each witness to understand the progression of the questioning, so testimony follows some logical order and has impact. The witnesses must be educated as to the process, how to talk, how to dress, what to say and what need not be said. The attorney gets to paint a picture, but not all the spaces in the picture have to be filled in. That's the job of the other side. Some things are better left unsaid.

Your testimony must be prepared. For every request you will make of the judge, the judge is required by statute to consider certain factors. Those factors are all listed in the state law books. You need to be familiarized with those factors, and all of the things you want to tell the judge must be pigeon-holed into the right spots, so your testimony flows right down the lists. You need to become very educated as to the law by your attorney, so you know what the judge wants to hear about, and what the judge does not want to hear about.

You also want to come across as likeable to the judge. Do you keep saying "my" son or "my" children, and not "our?" The court notices these things. The court will judge you, perhaps harshly. You probably won't fool the judge much. Chances are you and your spouse probably wouldn't be in court to begin with if both of you were reasonable, rational people. Judges know this.

All of the documents must be organized, copied and labeled. In some jurisdictions trial notebooks are required, wherein each side has an indexed listing of documents, and all of the documents are neatly arranged behind numbered tabs. Each lawyer, the judge and the witness on the stand all have a notebook from each side to refer to. Or instead, the attorneys may be operating with labeled folders, or with piles of papers with post-it labels attached.

Given that the documents in your case will typically easily fill at least two banker's boxes, and sometimes many more, it is vital that your attorney is organized, and knows exactly where each piece of paper is located. It is also important that the exhibits don't get all mixed up on the floor, if dropped in the crowded elevator by your attorney.

6. **Attorney Discussions**

Any offers of settlement made by one lawyer to the other lawyer, are supposed to be conveyed to the other party by his or her lawyer. If an attorney doesn't pass on a settlement offer, he or she is probably committing a violation of attorney ethics. Your attorneys may be trying to settle the case all the while it is being prepared, or a bad attorney may be trying his or her level best to prevent a settlement. Perhaps you will reach agreement on some of the issues, on some of the facts or as to some of the values. You may narrow the issues for trial.

The attorneys may agree to admit hearsay documents, such as appraisals and retirement statements, without forcing each other to subpoena for cross-examination the experts, or individuals known as "Custodians of Records," who prepared those documents. Or an attorney may wait to see if the other attorney remembered to file the necessary subpoenas for Custodians, and if that other attorney forgot, will happily make hearsay objections to try to keep important information out of evidence.

Your attorney may discuss strategy with you before the fact, or after. You may try to second guess the other side. Maybe your case will even settle sometime before trial. Maybe one or both lawyers are deliberately being obstinate, because of a determination to try the case. They may be determined to be your champion and to fight for your rights, or they may be determined to bill you for as much work as they can get away with.

7. **THE BIG DAY**

The night before THE BIG DAY you should try to get some sleep. The morning of THE BIG DAY you should eat, and you should drink some water. It isn't helpful to be fuzzy, incoherent or dizzy during the hearing. You may want to put some breath mints in your pocket, so when you lean over to whisper something important to your attorney during the trial, he or she doesn't back away.

You should know how to get to the courthouse, and through security, as should your witnesses. In some counties you may wait in line for more than half an hour to enter the building, only to learn that you must then go put your camera cell phone and nail clippers back in your car on the fourth floor of the parking garage, and that you will then have to get back in line. You need to know how to find your courtroom out of the maybe fifteen or so courtrooms located on three of the floors of the five storey building in the courthouse complex.

You may be asked to carry two of the four boxes of documents needed at trial. There may be one or two boxes of discovery documents and court papers, one box of trial notebooks and one box of legal references and trial notes for the attorney. You and your attorney each wheel your luggage carriers down the sidewalk, into the building, into the elevators and through the grand halls of the courthouse. You will feel that you must be very important, what with all of that information someone will be hearing all about.

Your attorney may have stayed up late into the night reviewing the pertinent case law, reviewing the evidence, and putting the finishing touches on the witness questions and on the opening statement. He or she also probably spent many late nights and weekends in the office the month before trial, making sure that discovery was supplemented on both sides, that all necessary witnesses and documents were subpoenaed, that all court exhibits were prepared and that all the calculations were done, checked, rechecked and checked again.

The bill you will get for all the work done by your attorney the month before trial will make your eyes pop.

8.   **The Hearing**

Now you all somberly file into the courtroom in your nice suits. The private certified verbatim court reporter is sworn in by the court clerk. The lawyers would have already argued over who should pay the appearance fee for the reporter's services. The judge's law clerk may be in the courtroom. The bailiffs are standing by, guns holstered, ready to tell you to remove your purse, bags and briefcase from the table, to keep your hands out of your pockets and that your cell phone will be confiscated if it goes off.

Your witnesses are all sworn in, and are then sent out into the hallway, with instructions not to discuss their testimony, to wait to be called back in later on in the day. Be sure to tell each of them to bring a book or a magazine, unless staggered times have been arranged for them to arrive. You may also instruct them not to glare too much at the other side's witnesses, not to make faces and comments once they finish testifying if they remain in the courtroom, and not to cause a scene at the end of the day, whichever way the case turns out.

The judge will inquire as to any "preliminary matters." There will always be something the lawyers will want to tell or ask the judge right before getting started. Then you will get started.

Each side makes an opening statement. The first side calls a witness to testify. That witness may then be cross-examined. There may be some testimony on redirect in response to the cross-examination. All of the first side's witnesses are called and cross-examined, perhaps with some redirect, one by one.

You will discover that blood is thicker than water, and that to your surprise, your in-laws may not be all that helpful to your case. You will learn which of your and your spouse's "mutual" friends really aren't. You will hear lies.

The other side then calls witnesses one by one for testimony and cross-examination. The first side may call rebuttal witnesses, who may also be cross-examined. Objections fly right and left, rulings are made sustaining and overruling the objections, tears are shed, documents are introduced and admitted into evidence or excluded, and the judge may ask a question or two.

After the last document and last word of testimony is submitted, each side may present a closing argument. Or if it is too late in the day, the judge may ask for written closing statements. If written closing statements are requested, your attorney will go back to the office, and will spend a lot of time summarizing the evidence, making arguments and preparing a nice long document for the judge to read. He or she will bill you for all of that time.

The trial may be one day long, two days long or longer, unless you got bumped by an emergency case that had to be heard immediately, and you had to reschedule. You may start at 9:00 a.m. or later each day, and will end at 4:00 or 5:00 p.m. each day. There will be a break of about one hour each day for lunch. If your trial is more than one day long, your attorney, and possibly you, will be working late into the night after each day of trial, locating and preparing rebuttal evidence.

9. <u>The Rulings</u>

The judge may present rulings verbally right at the end of the hearing, or may take the matter "under advisement." If the judge does not rule right away, you may have to come back another day to hear the rulings, or the judge and his or her law clerk may prepare a letter opinion, and fax it to both counsel.

It is the perception of most divorce attorneys that most judges rule in a consistent way on similar facts. That is a nice way of saying that the judge's mind was already made up before you even entered the courtroom. While your and your spouse's views are clouded by one-sided outlooks and by emotion, judges base their rulings upon the principles which they believe should govern in situations such as yours.

It is also the perception of many divorce attorneys that most judges really don't want to hear ugly divorce suits, and will try hard to encourage you to settle. We have that perception because the judges tell us that you, and not they, should decide how to parent your children, that neither of you will be entirely happy with the result of a trial, that you will each pay a fortune to fight with each other through your attorneys when you could instead use that money for your family, and that high conflict divorces cause irreparable harm to your children. Often they will see your children a few years later, on the days the criminal docket is heard. They know that your children, your children's children, and society as a whole, will be the casualties of your little war.

So the reality is that somewhere along the way, whether before, during or just after opening statements, or somewhere during the trial, the judge made up his or her mind on some of the facts and on the crucial main facts, and then just listened to the rest of the case to hear whether or not there was a good reason to change that opinion.

Then the judge will issue his or her rulings. Simply with the delivery of those rulings, however, you are not yet done. "The court speaks through its orders."

10. The Order

One of the attorneys must then write the judge's rulings into one or more court orders. There may be a comprehensive final decree of divorce, or separate orders on property, spousal support, custody and child support. Pension orders may have to be prepared.

Before the written final decree of divorce is submitted to the judge for entry, you must decide if you want to appeal anything. If you do, your specific objections must be written into the order that the judge will sign. If you don't object to the specific rulings with which you disagree at the time the judge signs the order, preserving those particular objections, you can't appeal.

If the judge made verbal rulings, and if the two attorneys disagree over the wording of the proposed written order, the private certified verbatim court reporter must be paid to prepare a transcript of the court's rulings, and everyone goes back to court with a copy of that expensive transcript to clarify with the judge exactly what he or she said, or to clarify what the words actually meant. It was mentioned earlier on in this *Guide* that attorneys can argue both sides of anything. They can also find anything to argue about.

Eventually, an order or orders will be prepared that everyone can agree upon, or must accept, and which the judge will enter. When the pen is lifted from the paper, you are divorced. Yay!

11. **Are We Done?**

No.

As long as there is no Motion for a Rehearing, or Motion to Reconsider, and assuming neither of you have filed an appeal, now you have to implement the rulings. Property must be sold, refinanced, conveyed or divided. A new deed to the former marital home may need to be prepared, to avoid unintended survivorship or inheritance consequences. If you die after you are divorced without a Will, before retitling the former marital home, your new spouse and your ex-spouse could each own half of that home together. How cozy. Visitation arrangements must be put into effect. Payroll withholding orders for support may have to be entered, and pension funds may have to be transferred.

And THE FINAL BILL must be paid to each attorney for all of the fine hard work done on your behalf, regardless of whether you "won" or "lost." If you don't pay, you may find yourself after the word "versus" before the word "Defendant" in a suit to recover attorney's fees. Your attorney's name will be on the other side of the "v."

Then, after having gone through all of that, if you and your now ex-spouse have children together, you will have to sit with each other at their graduations and at their weddings, and you will have to smile happily for the cameras. The looks on your faces will express the wreckage your family has become.

Was it worth it? Will you ever remarry? Will you now marry the "paramour" and drift happily off into the sunset? If so, get a Prenuptial Agreement done, so that you don't have to go through all of this ever again.

ᏣᎳ

CONCLUSION

It is my sincere hope that the preceding pages have shown you that all need not be bleak. You do have some measure of control. Hopefully, a great deal of control.

I have come to see from the thousands of people I have worked with over the years, that much of the discord in our lives is of our own creation, and it is passed from one generation to the next.

You can be a wonderful and memorable example and inspiration to your children, to others and to yourself, if you act smartly, firmly and graciously. Or not.

I often tell new clients sitting in my office for the first time, that I go through boxes of tissues each year, handing them out to both my male and female clients. When I first meet those with whom I work, they are usually in about the lowest place they will be emotionally during the divorce process.

I then often tell my clients that I see many of my former clients, years after their divorces are over, for reasons such as adjusting support, doing estate planning, creating a business or by their just dropping by to say "Hi" or to tell me they have referred a friend or family member to my office. Often we run into each other about town.

I then tell my clients, as I hand them more tissues, that virtually without exception, everyone I meet years later is doing so much better than they were when they first came to see me. Even if their spouses had cheated on them and left them, even if they had been homemakers for thirty years and had never held a job, even if the time they spend with their children was redefined and the family was restructured, and even if they had to move from the big single family home into a much smaller place, that cloud of unhappiness did go away, and life got brighter.

It will get brighter for you too.

You will have some rough spots at first, and the process can take about two years. You may have to move, live apart from your spouse for a year, rent a room or apartment for awhile, sell a home, buy a home or refinance a home, change jobs or increase your work hours, get used to shuttling the children back and forth and to being there for them when they have extra needs, get documents negotiated and signed or obtain administrative child support or court orders, complete the actual divorce case and get out from under all the legal fees. You may even have to go through a bankruptcy.

But there is light at the end of the tunnel. You will be happy again, and you will get your finances under control again, even if it seems you never possibly could. You will. You will not view your children as from a "broken" home, but now of *two* homes.

You may even forgive your spouse. You may find that to do so lifts a weight of negativity off you that you no longer have to carry around.

I hope you will use this *Guide* to help you seek the right type of legal professional, and to help you ask that professional the right questions. I hope you will use this *Guide* to work with your legal professional, and with the other necessary professionals, to decide together upon the best course of action for your needs, based upon your state's current laws and upon your special circumstances.

Divorce is a pothole in the road of life. Look through the windshield as you go, and not at the rearview. Divorce should only be an event in your life, and should not define who you are. Your divorce will provide you with an opportunity for personal and spiritual growth. Take that opportunity to act in a noble way, and to become a better person.

Your true colors will come out in adversity. So will your spouse's. And how you each deal with the other will define you as either selfish, petty, small-hearted, mean-spirited and cruel, or as respectful, dignified, compassionate, caring and firm.

I hope this *Guide* will help you and your family opt for the latter. You'll all be a lot happier. You owe it to yourself, and to the children you chose to bring into the world.

There really are no social constructs regarding how one should properly go about getting a divorce. I would offer the following six principles:

1. Be your best. Conduct yourself honorably, truthfully and as an example to others.

2. Put your children first. Make decisions about your new life that are in their best interests, and not only in yours.

3. Take care of yourself mentally, physically and spiritually.

4. Be smart about ensuring and working towards a financially secure future.

5. Act in a socially responsible way. Don't create dysfunctional children who will become a drain on society.

6. Remain optimistic about the future.

Litigation will hurt you and your family. Compromise is better than combat. If you can work it all out, it will work out for all of you. Try to stay out of court.

Good luck, and blessings to you.

APPENDIX 1

COMPARISON CHART OF LITIGATION, NEGOTIATION, COLLABORATION AND MEDIATION

	Litigation	Negotiation	Collaboration	Mediation
You have an attorney advocating your interests	Yes	Yes	Yes	Only if your attorney participates in and accompanies you to the mediation, or if you consult with an attorney outside the process. But the mediator is neutral.
The attorney can go to court with you	Yes	Yes	The collaborative attorney can only file uncontested matters, and can not go to court with you in a contested case.	The mediator can't, but if you have a separate attorney, that attorney can.

167

continuation of COMPARISON CHART OF

LITIGATION, NEGOTIATION, COLLABORATION AND MEDIATION

	Litigation	Negotiation	Collaboration	Mediation
You will be in court	Yes	Maybe. At any time during negotiations, suit can be filed. Negotiation can also occur at any time during a litigated case.	Only if you terminate the collaborative process and retain new counsel for court.	Maybe. Mediation can be undertaken at any time before a case is filed, or after.
$ Cost $	Usually the most costly of the four processes.	Can be costly.	Usually less costly than litigation, and usually more costly than mediation.	Usually the least costly overall.
You have control over the process	You have some control, but the ultimate result is up to a judge.	You can decide what to settle for.	You can decide what to settle for.	You can decide what to settle for.

continuation of COMPARISON CHART OF

LITIGATION, NEGOTIATION, COLLABORATION AND MEDIATION

	Litigation	Negotiation	Collaboration	Mediation
Decisions are made in accordance with "the law"	Yes, or at least in accordance with the judge's interpretation of the law.	The negotiations may be based on what would happen in court, but don't have to be.	You are free to create your own solution.	You are free to create your own solution.
Level of animosity	The highest potential to foster animosity exists.	Less likely to have a high level than with litigation, but still some potential for animosity.	Active emphasis on minimizing animosity.	Animosity is unlikely to occur when lawyers are not a part of the mediation.
Creates healing and generates goodwill	QUITE the opposite!	Only if as a by-product of the process.	Strong focus on creating and maintaining goodwill.	The focus is firmly on creating and maintaining goodwill when lawyers are not a part of the mediation.

APPENDIX 2

FINANCIAL WORKSHEET FORMS

Worksheet for: _____

1. **Bank accounts.** Provide the following information for all bank accounts such as checking accounts, savings accounts, credit union accounts or certificates of deposit, established in your name individually or in joint names with any other:

Name of bank or other institution	Type of account	In whose name	Balance at separation	Present balance
			$	$
			$	$
			$	$
			$	$
			$	$

2. **Investment accounts.** Provide the following information for any money market accounts, mutual fund accounts, stocks, bonds, IRAs or other investment accounts owned by you individually or jointly with any other, including stock options:

Name of institution	Type of account	By whom owned	Original deposit or cost	Present value
			$	$
			$	$
			$	$
			$	$
			$	$
			$	$

3. Defined contribution retirement accounts. Provide the following information for any *defined contribution* retirement plan (where the value of the plan is defined by the "bottom line" in your most recent statement). These include TSP, 401k or 403b plans, profit sharing plans and other tax deferred retirement investments or accounts owned by you individually, for which the amount of your interest is defined by the contributions made by you or on your behalf:

Name of institution	Type of account (ex. TSP, 401k)	By whom owned	Amount of orig. deposit/ cost	Present value
			$	$
			$	$
			$	$
			$	$
			$	$
			$	$

4. Defined benefit retirement plans. Provide the following information for any *defined benefit* retirement plan (a plan based upon a formula which takes into account your years of service and average high salary at the end) to which you are entitled to receive by virtue of your past or current employment:

Name of plan	Date service commenced	Date service ended	Contributions paid in
	(Month, day, yr.) / /	(Month, day, yr.) / /	$
	(Month, day, yr.) / /	(Month, day, yr.) / /	$
Years in plan to date	**Age when full benefits start**	**Projected retirement date**	**Expected monthly income**
	(Month, day, yr.) / /	(Month, day, yr.) / /	$
	(Month, day, yr.) / /	(Month, day, yr.) / /	$

5. Real estate. For any real estate titled in your name individually or jointly with any other (including single family homes, town homes, condominiums, timeshares etc.) provide the following information:

Location (address)	S/f, t/h, condo	How titled	Original cost	When bought	Due on loan(s)	Present value
			$		$	$
			$		$	$
			$		$	$

6. Life insurance. Provide the following information for any life insurance policies owned by you or which name you as a beneficiary:

Insurance company	Type of policy	Whose life	Owner	Beneficiaries	Face value	Cash value
					$	$
					$	$
					$	$

7. Business or professional interests. Provide the following information for any business or professional entities or interests which are owned by you individually or jointly with any other:

Business or professional name	Legal status (S Corp., LLC)	% owned	Amount invested	Value of your interest
			$	$
			$	$

Nature of business	When established	Gross annual income		Annual profit
		$		$
		$		$

8.   Household items. List the major items or categories of household furnishings or personal effects having an estimated value in excess of $500 per item or general category (such as china, silver, antiques, firearms, original art, oriental rugs, collections, jewelry and furs) which are owned by you individually or jointly with any other:

Nature of item	Owner(s)	Where located	Original cost	Estimated value
			$	$
			$	$
			$	$
			$	$
			$	$
			$	$

9.   Vehicles, etc. Provide the following information regarding any automobiles, trucks, motorcycles, boats, personal watercraft, airplanes or other vehicles, which are titled in your name individually or which are jointly titled with any other:

Year	Description (model/ type)	How titled	Purchase price	Amount due on loan	Estimated value
			$	$	$
			$	$	$
			$	$	$
			$	$	$

10. **Increase or decrease in value**. As to any **substantial** increase or decrease in the value of any item of real or personal property listed in Items 1-9 above since the property was acquired, provide the following information:

Description of property	When acquired	Purchase price	Estimated value	Reason for change
		$	$	
		$	$	
		$	$	
		$	$	

11. **Credit accounts**. Provide the following information for your current credit cards, personal charge accounts, credit loans and loans and notes payable, including those in your name alone or jointly with any other:

Creditor	Why incurred	When incurred	Account number	Person(s) liable	Present balance
					$
					$
					$
					$
					$
					$
					$
					$
					$
					$

12. Separate property. List any property which you consider to be your separate property, in that you possessed the property at the time of the marriage, or acquired the property after the marriage through a gift from a third party (not your spouse) or from an inheritance, or property which you acquired after the date of any final separation:

Nature of item	When acquired	From	Gift, inher., premarital	How titled	Estimated value
					$
					$
					$
					$
					$

13. Changes in property. Are there any assets valued in excess of $500 titled in your name, either individually or jointly with any other, which have been acquired or disposed of since the date of your separation? If so, provide the following information:

Description	Owner(s)	Acquired or disposed of	Why	When	Cost or amt. received
					$
					$
					$
					$
					$
					$
					$
					$

14. Employers. Give the name of each of your current employers, and for each employment provide the following information:

Employer	Position	Years of service	Pay period	Annual salary
				$
				$

15. Other income. State any additional source of employment or consulting income, including any bonuses in your current position, and for each provide the following information:

Source of income	Nature of position or type of income	Estimated income	Monthly or annual

16. Gross income and deductions. What is your pay period - monthly, every two weeks (biweekly), twice monthly (semi-monthly), weekly or other? State your average income and deductions from your primary employment for each *pay period*:

Pay period	Gross pay	Federal taxes	State taxes	FICA	Retirement
	$	$	$	$	$
Prof. dues	**Overtime**	**Health insurance**	**Life insurance**	**Other deductions**	**Net income**
$	$	$	$	$	$

17. **Secondary employment**. State your average income and deductions from any secondary employment for each pay period:

Pay period	Gross pay	Federal taxes	State taxes	FICA	Retirement
	$	$	$	$	$
Prof. dues	**Overtime**	**Health insurance**	**Life insurance**	**Other deductions**	**Net income**
$	$	$	$	$	$

18. **Tax exemptions**. State the number and names of all persons you claim as income tax exemptions: **no. of exemptions** [   ]; names ___

_____

_____

19. **Other sources of income**. State your average net monthly income from any other source, such as dividends, interest, trust income, rental income and royalties.

Source of income	When received	How often	Estimated monthly amount
			$
			$
			$
			$
			$
			$
			$

20.   Health insurance, dental plan and optical plan coverage. Furnish the following information concerning the primary and any secondary health insurance coverage for the family, including coverage through the military:

Name of carrier	Type of plan	Persons covered	Monthly cost	Plan number

Added cost to add spouse and/or child/ren – the difference between the monthly cost for a policy covering the insured's spouse and/or child/ren, and the monthly cost for an individual policy for the insured IF the insured had self-only coverage (check with the employer for what that cost would be):

(family plan cost minus self-only plan cost = cost to add spouse and/or child/ren: $ _____)

21.   Safe deposit boxes. If there are any safe deposit boxes, vaults, safes or other places of deposit or safekeeping in which you have stored any money, financial documents such as stock certificates or bonds, coins, jewelry or other items of personal property, during the past two years, please state the location, and describe all items previously or presently deposited:

Location	Items deposited	When deposited	Estimated value
			$
			$

22.   Property held for your benefit. If any person, firm or other entity holds any property for your benefit, describe the property in full, including the name and address of the holder, and a description of and the value of the property:

Holder	Address	Reason held	Nature of property	Estimated value
				$
				$

23.   Debts owed to you. For any outstanding notes, accounts receivable or other debts owed **to you** individually, or to you with any other, provide the following information:

By whom payable	Reason for obligation	To whom payable	Rate of interest	Due date	Amount due
					$
					$

24.   Other investments. Provide the following information for any land investments, partnerships, joint ventures or any other such investments owned by you individually or jointly with any other:

Description	% owned	Title	Invested	When	Value
			$		$
			$		$
			$		$

APPENDIX 3

INFORMATIVE MEDIATION –
A NEW MODEL FOR TOUGH ECONOMIC TIMES

This article is reprinted from when it first appeared in the fall 2008 issue of <u>Family Law News</u> *published by the Family Law Section of the Virginia State Bar Association*

Some couples going through a divorce are rational, intelligent, honorable, generous and strongly focused on trying to create the best possible futures for their children as a two-home family. In some cases, even where there has been adultery and betrayal, and even where one of the parties has struggled with depression or substance abuse, **some individuals don't hate each other just because they are getting a divorce.**

I have been litigating divorce cases throughout Northern Virginia since 1989, and half of my practice is still litigation. However, unlike those of my colleagues who are focused almost entirely on winning the battle in court, it has also been my honor and privilege since 2001 to assist divorcing couples in amicably mediating their divorces.

There do exist individuals who face the restructuring of their lives and family with honor and integrity. There do exist individuals who wish to exemplify for their children, by example, how to deal with the sadness and tragedy life can offer at times. There do exist individuals who understand that divorce, as any adverse circumstance, can bring out either the best or the worst in a person. There do exist individuals who rise to the challenge of doing what is right, given the circumstances, for the family.

These are the people my firm markets to – people who want to handle the legalities of their divorce without adversity. People who do not wish to resolve their disputes the old-fashioned way, which is by hiring two lawyers to put on a show for a judge. People who understand that lawyers can argue both sides of anything, including *Brandenburg, Keeling,* and the related cases. People who understand that the judge will find a way to do whatever he or she feels is just. Just like squeezing a balloon - squeeze here, but it comes out there. Get what you want as to the valuation of an asset, but get hit on spousal support or attorney's fees.

Not everyone distrusts or has reason to distrust his or her spouse in a divorce. Not everyone needs an advocate to actively and adversarially negotiate, but instead can use the attorney in his or her corner for advice, for information and for document reviews. Not everyone needs to pay for a two-attorney collaborative process. Not everyone wants to duplicate the costs and effort in obtaining the assistance of experts "for each side."

How can a divorce attorney best serve this market? Through the process of Informative Mediation, summarized and described below.

SUMMARY OF THE INFORMATIVE MEDIATION PROCESS

<u>Step One</u>. The paralegal identifies and screens for appropriate participants.

<u>Step Two</u>. The paralegal sets the initial appointment and sends the clients a Topics List.

<u>**Step Three.**</u>   **The Informative Mediator conducts the Initial Session.**

     A. In the Informative Mediation model, as in all models of mediation, during the initial session the mediator describes the style of the mediation and the usual progression of the process.

>   1. **In Informative Mediation the clients are told during the initial session that most simple Informative Mediations are completed within three to five two-hour sessions.**

>   2. **In Informative Mediation the clients are told during the initial session that they will each be fully informed as to the law throughout the process.**

>   3. **In Informative Mediation the clients are told during the initial session that "what the law is" is arguable. The goal of Informative Mediation is that if the clients each have their Mediated Agreement reviewed by individual attorneys on each of their behalf before signing, they each receive no further legal information that they did not receive during the mediation.**

>   4. **Because what individual attorneys advising each client might tell them relates to how the local judges have been ruling lately, the clients are told during the initial session of the Informative Mediation that there is an expectation they are asking for an evaluative component to the mediation, and that they will receive evaluative information.**

>   5. **The clients are told during the initial session of an Informative Mediation, that if and as appropriate, the mediator may at times present a variety of options which have worked for others in similar situations, but will not unethically advise the clients to take any particular course of action.**

6.   The clients are asked if they have any questions.

B.   The Agreement to Mediate is discussed briefly during the initial session, paragraph by paragraph, and any questions of the clients' are answered.

C.   The mediator asks brief background questions during the initial session, in order to gain an understanding of the clients' situation.

D.   Because they will be signing a Mediated Agreement at the conclusion of the process, the clients are told during the initial session of an Informative Mediation what a contract is, and what a contract isn't.

E.   The remainder of the initial session is then spent addressing each item on the Topics List.

F.   The Informative Mediation Model considers the restructuring of the family as a whole.

G.   The clients may decide at the conclusion of the initial session that they wish to gather additional information, either from their own sources, or by referral to other members of the mediator's "team."

Step Four.   The Informative Mediator helps the clients to propose, to evaluate and to agree on options, usually during the second session.

Step Five.   The Informative Mediator writes down the points of agreement, usually during the last session.

Step Six.   The Informative Mediator explains the meaning of the boilerplate language which will be included in the Mediated

Agreement, and the choices within that language, during the last session.

Step Seven. The Informative Mediator explains the actual divorce process to the clients during the last session.

Step Eight. The Informative Mediator drafts the Agreement.

Step Nine. The Mediated Agreement is scanned and sent to each client.

Step Ten. The Informative Mediator prepares any necessary retirement orders, military DD forms and transmittal letters, after receipt of a copy of the signed Mediated Agreement from the clients.

Step Eleven. The Informative Mediator sends closing letters to the clients.

DESCRIPTION OF THE INFORMATIVE MEDIATION PROCESS

Step One. The paralegal identifies and screens for appropriate participants.

Many potential divorce clients know they will not go to court, and wish to settle their cases amicably. However, there may be some issues to resolve, such as: marital and separate components of assets to be teased out, perhaps earnings on those separate assets to be calculated, stock options to be valued, properties to be appraised, some haggling over an amount and duration for alimony, a custodial schedule to be discussed and worked out and child support to be calculated. Perhaps even a business or professional practice to be valued. Some of these individuals merely need guidance.

When a prospective client calls the office, the first and most crucial step is for the experienced paralegal to discuss *The Four Ways of Divorce* with that person, to determine whether he or she needs to stand up for himself or herself through *litigation*, whether the process must be an adversarial *negotiation*, whether the client and his or her spouse may be good candidates for *mediation*, or whether the client and his or her spouse may truly both want to settle amicably out of court, but one or both of the parties needs an advocate to give voice to his or her concerns through *collaboration*.

Questions must be asked regarding feelings of safety, the ability to discuss concerns on an equal basis, any previous proceedings involving physical abuse, and whether there are any mental health or substance abuse issues. While no one of the above concerns *per se* rules out mediation, the mediator must have the experience and expertise to properly conduct a mediation involving any such circumstances. If questions arise related to an individual's ability to meaningfully participate in mediation, collaboration may be an option for those who would have an even more difficult time handling the rigors of litigation.

The first individual to discuss the process with the paralegal is told to ask his or her spouse to also call the office, so the same information can be conveyed, and so there is no perception that the firm somehow has the interests of the first person at heart. During these calls with the paralegal, the paralegal merely discusses how the mediation would progress, but does not ask for details of the situation, and does not convey information to the mediator, so as to avoid the creation of any bias or preconceived ideas on the mediator's part.

Step Two. **The paralegal sets the initial appointment and sends the clients a Topics List.**

An initial appointment is set, blocking three hours on the calendar. The initial session is usually about two and one-half hours long. A comprehensive Topics List is sent to the clients in advance of the meeting for them to consider. A purely facilitative mediator might say that "if the clients didn't think of an issue the mediator shouldn't raise it," due to worries of "interfering with the clients' self-determination." Conversely, the very purpose of Informative Mediation is *specifically* to let the clients know what they need to think about, such as mortgage interest deductions, any capital loss carryovers, life insurance and estate planning, the division of any flex fund benefits, the meaning and choices within boilerplate language, along with the usual basic concerns such as custody, visitation, support and the division of retirement and other marital assets. The clients are then free to decide themselves how they wish to resolve these important matters, with the assistance of the mediator.

The more matters the clients can discuss and agree upon together, and the more prepared they are, the less time-consuming (costly) the mediation process will be. The clients are each told that if, however, discussion of any hot button items causes discord, they should save discussion of those matters for the mediation sessions, and in any case, to never discuss substantive issues in front of their children.

Step Three.   The Informative Mediator conducts the Initial Session.

In the reception area the clients will each fill out Intake Sheets which include screening questions. Once these are completed, the paralegal will bring those sheets back to the mediator to review. The mediator reviews this information as the clients are given and review the Agreement to Mediate, while still in the reception area. If any concerns arise as a result of the mediator's review of the written screening questions, the mediator must address them. If the paralegal is knowledgeable and spoke in advance to both clients, concerns will rarely arise once the clients are in the office. The mediator will then bring the clients (and drinks for them) into the room to begin the process. The session may be conducted in the mediator's office with the mediator behind his or her desk, or at a large table.

A.   In the Informative Mediation model, as in all models of mediation, during the initial session the mediator describes the style of the mediation and the usual progression of the process. The mediator will state that the clients are engaged in the process of Informative Mediation, and will then describe what Informative Mediation is. The clients will be told that during the initial session the following will occur: the way the mediation will be conducted will be discussed, that what is typical in terms of numbers of sessions for the process and what typically is done in each session will be discussed, that the clients will go over and sign the Agreement to Mediate with the mediator, that the mediator will then ask some brief background questions, that the Topics List will be addressed, that determinations will be made of any need to collect further information, and that appropriate referrals may be made to neutral professionals who have a trusted relationship with the mediator to assist the clients in obtaining that information. These points are described more fully below.

In addition, the mediator should also make clear that he or she does not represent either party or both parties, that it is unethical for the mediator to *advise* either or both parties, and that he or she can not and will not be filing the actual divorce suit when the mediation is concluded.

1.   In Informative Mediation the clients are told during the initial session that most simple Informative Mediations can be completed within three to five two-hour sessions: the initial session described in this article; a second session to go over information which has been collected, to discuss various actions and individual goals based on that information, and to look at and resolve any differences; and a third session to clarify all agreements reached so as to prepare the Mediated Agreement, to discuss the actual filing of a divorce case, and to go over the meaning of the boilerplate language which will be included in the Mediated Agreement and the choices within that language. If the situation is complex, or if the clients have many disagreements or difficulties, the "second session" may perhaps take two or three meetings. If a mediation is not concluded after about five two-hour sessions, the issues are either extraordinarily complex, or the case may not settle appropriately through mediation.

The clients will be told that they will pay for the time spent at the end of each mediation session before they leave, and that they will put down a deposit before the Mediated Agreement is drafted. An advanced fee deposit may not be necessary because many individuals come in just prior to or just after their separation, when they are unsure as to how to proceed, and after the initial session they may frequently return five to seven months later to finalize matters after having completed much of the work to be done. Others set less time between sessions and may work quickly to get their Agreement prepared. Since there is no work which the mediator need do between sessions in the office, and the mediator does not communicate with either or both clients outside of the sessions, it is therefore appropriate for the clients to simply "pay as they go."

In a process of trust, where there are no issues involving substance abuse, gambling or other wasting of assets, the clients may decide to buy, sell, refinance, pay off, divide and otherwise work towards a separation of their assets, even before their Agreement is signed. If the mediation were to fail, the use of and transfer of assets can be traced and argued should the matter be litigated, without prejudice or harm to the parties. In many cases there is no need for the clients to wait for the drafting and endorsement of an Agreement before moving forward with the final financial and physical separation.

2.   In Informative Mediation the clients are told during the initial session that they will each be fully informed as to the law throughout the process. The clients are involved in a legal process. The goal of that process is for the clients to sign a legally binding, enforceable contract at the conclusion of the process. Accordingly, since each client must be informed as to "the law," neutral information on all relevant topics is provided during the mediation.

In my practice I also invite the clients to attend the free monthly informational seminar I have been conducting since approximately 2000. By receiving information in a general setting, any perception of bias over the contents of that information, such as information regarding how local judges typically rule in custody and visitation cases, may be alleviated.

3.   In Informative Mediation the clients are told during the initial session that "what the law is" is arguable. Because "what the law is" can be a bit subjective and subject to interpretation and argument, it follows that competing views should be presented during the mediation for balance. In the Informative Mediation model each client is given, right in front of the other, the information which attorneys separately representing each person would likely provide each of them. The ethical line of individually *advising* must never be crossed, however, or the mediator may find him or herself in hot water. The attorney mediator is also ethically prohibited from engaging in any sort of duel representation, and should not be advising the clients collectively, either.

Information should simply be given out in a neutral, unbiased manner. But even if five or ten of fifteen points of law favor one client's views, conveying that information does not make the mediator biased. It is what it is. **The goal of Informative Mediation is that if the clients each have their Mediated Agreement reviewed by individual attorneys on each of their behalf before signing, they each receive no further legal information that they did not receive during the mediation.** By way of example, the clients may make significant provision for the post-secondary education of their children, knowing full well that their individual attorneys will tell each of them that no Virginia judge could make either of them pay for college. The goal is for the response to be, "Yes, the mediator told us that."

4.   Because what individual attorneys working with each client might tell them relates to how the local judges have been ruling lately, the clients are told during the initial session of the Informative Mediation that there is an expectation they are asking for an evaluative component to the mediation, and that they will receive evaluative information. The mediator of course must be qualified to conduct an evaluative mediation. Many intelligent, computer savvy clients attempt on their own to educate themselves as to "the law." But the "local law" may involve Income and Expense Sheets, and local *Pendente Lite* Spousal Support Guidelines, which the clients will be unlikely to find on the internet. Information regarding recent trends in local rulings is best conveyed by a mediator who is also an experienced, qualified, locally practicing litigator.

5.   The clients are told during the initial session of an Informative Mediation, that if and as appropriate, the mediator may at times present a variety of options which have worked for others in similar situations, but will not unethically *advise* the clients to take any particular course of action. By contrast, a truly facilitative mediator may be reluctant to suggest, for example, that if a conflict arises as to each client's choice of summer vacation weeks with the children, some two-home families find it useful that in odd numbered years one parent's choice shall have priority, and the other's in even numbered years. Or that some divorced or separated parents who get along quite well, who were married for decades, who will continue to reside near each other and who have well-adjusted older children, do quite well with a custodial schedule such as Monday and Tuesday with Mom, Wednesday and Thursday with Dad, and Friday through Sunday being alternated.

Mediation is an art and not a science. The mediator will call upon his or her training, experience and skill to guide the clients through the process of clarifying and deciding upon which options the clients feel are most appropriate for their situation.

6. The clients are asked if they have any questions. The mediator will "check in" with each client after each topic is addressed, to ensure the clients understand how the mediation will be conducted.

B. The Agreement to Mediate is discussed briefly during the initial session, paragraph by paragraph, and any questions of the clients' are answered. Discussion of the content of the Agreement to Mediate is outside the scope of this article, but topics such as the requirement of absolute full disclosure, confidentiality and third-party involvement are addressed. One copy of the Agreement will then be signed and given to the paralegal, who will make copies of the fully endorsed Agreement for each client. The other two copies will be collected and reused in the future for another case.

C. The mediator asks brief background questions during the initial session, in order to gain an understanding of the clients' situation. Starting with one individual, each client's age, previous states of residence, location of other supportive family members, education and employment history and earnings history will be ascertained. The clients will be asked if their children have any special needs, and in what if any activities their children participate. The clients may each be asked how they envision living their lives two or five years in the future.

Then the clients will each be invited to briefly state what brings them to the mediation – "Who got unhappy first?" It is expressed by the mediator that the purpose of the mediation is not to settle who's "at fault," since lawyers can usually find a way to argue there is some fault on both sides, but "What is the Reader's Digest version of what brings you here?" During Informative Mediation discussions, however, any impact relating to fault will be discussed in an evaluative light.

The question is asked so the mediator can ascertain and clarify where the clients each are on the denial, bargaining, grief, anger, acceptance stages of the dissolution of the marriage. If one client is still in denial over the ending of the marriage, or if one or both of the clients are still stuck in the anger stage, the mediation will probably not succeed. Each client is asked point blank if he or she wants a divorce, and not "just a separation." Occasionally this mediation session is the first time one client hears that the other truly wants a divorce. In these cases, the initial session will often end after some discussion that one client in fact does want the divorce, because the other client has not yet had time to process this information, and to fully evaluate his or her options.

It is important to establish that both clients are truly on board with the idea that they are getting a divorce. It is important to ensure that one client does not feel he or she is simply working towards signing a document that won't mean anything, because he or she believes there will be a reconciliation. Of course the purpose of Informative Mediation is not to undertake marriage counseling or otherwise counsel the clients towards either a reconciliation or a divorce. However, the reality of divorce must have already been achieved and comprehended by both clients for the mediation to be appropriate, and that is simply the point that must be briefly ascertained and established.

D.   Because they will be signing a Mediated Agreement at the conclusion of the process, the clients are told during the initial session of an Informative Mediation what a contract is, and what a contract isn't. A non-lawyer mediator is prohibiting from engaging in the unauthorized practice of law. He or she may draft a "Memorandum of Understanding," which the clients may or may not then sign on their own. A non-lawyer purely facilitative mediator may not even tell the clients whether or not a binding contract is created if they put their signatures to that document, as he or she may be concerned that he or she is "giving legal advice."

By contrast, an attorney Informative Mediator will prepare a binding, enforceable contract, and will so inform the clients. The clients will be told that the contract can be as detailed and as specific as they would like, or as general as they would like. Together the clients can create their own separate futures the way they would like to live them.

The clients will also be informed that they can address as many future contingencies as they wish, with specificity, but will never be able to predict all the possibilities which may occur. For example, in discussing the maintenance and repair of a marital property to be listed for sale or held in one client's name for some period of time, there could occur a basement flood which may or may not have been due to the negligence of the occupant, who did not turn off the outdoor faucet before the pipes froze and burst, or a tree could fall on the home. Provision may be made for repairs to be shared if not due to the negligence of a client, but not everything may be foreseen.

The difference between binding provisions and aspirational provisions will also be discussed. If the clients wish to include aspirational provisions in areas such as agreement on extracurricular expenses for children, the payment of college expenses, and the filing of joint tax returns provided they can agree as to the allocation of any refund or further liability, they must understand that if they do not attain that aspirational goal, the provision is not legally binding.

E.   The remainder of the initial session is then spent addressing each item on the Topics List. The purpose of spending a minute or two on each of the thirty or so topics is not to see "What the clients have agreed to" or what they are each hoping for, but to ascertain whether: 1) the topic even applies, such as whether there are any investment properties or businesses, 2) whether the clients have already reached agreement on the issue (without yet getting into what that agreement *is*), 3) whether the clients would like legal and/or evaluative information on the topic, 4) whether the clients would like for options to be presented for the resolution of the topic, 5) whether more information should be obtained before the topic can be resolved, such as values for a former marital home and other assets, or 6) whether the topic will require some work if it is to be resolved. The mediator and the clients will then have a clearer idea of the conflict level, and of how the mediation will need to progress.

F.   The Informative Mediation Model considers the restructuring of the family as a whole. Adversarial litigation and negotiation do not typically address the overall needs of the restructuring of the two-home family, nor many of the individual needs of clients with or without children. Informative Mediation is a more holistic process. Accordingly, it may be suggested that the clients obtain further information and/or advice from other individuals, as described below, before decisions can be finalized and an Agreement drafted.

G.   The clients may decide at the conclusion of the initial session that they wish to gather additional information, either from their own sources, or by referral to other members of the mediator's "team." For example, a first task may be to appraise the former marital home and to then consult with a mortgage lender, to see if one individual is able to qualify to refinance and buy out the other client's equity. A mother who is still caring in the home for the children, by agreement of the parties, may need a referral to an individual who can assist her in obtaining health insurance post-divorce. To address the possible loss of support due to the death or disability of the payor, or to alleviate some concerns over future medical and financial needs, information may be gathered regarding the costs for life insurance, for disability insurance, and/or for a long-term care policy from the appropriate agents. Since it may not be the best option to designate young children directly on a life insurance beneficiary form, it may be a good idea to create a testamentary or living trust. Referral may then be made to an estate-planning attorney for the appropriate advice.

Mediation in general, at its best, concerns itself with what will work best for all involved, and not with who can grab more of the marbles. Informative Mediation in particular looks beyond the mere legal analysis, to also address the non-legal needs of the clients and children. For example, although usually not as great a need in mediation as in litigation, the clients may want to discuss the use of a parenting coordinator to assist them with communication issues in the future. In addition, one individual still struggling with the ending of the marriage may benefit from receiving a list of recommended mental health therapists from the mediator.

Significantly, in cases where overall tax consequences and professional fees can be minimized, the parties can meet together with a **licensed financial planner trained in divorce concerns and alternative dispute resolution**, so as to mutually evaluate various financial scenarios. These appropriately trained professionals, with guidance and explanation from the mediator, can perform strictly financial analyses such as the calculation of values of marital and separate interests, can analyze the various ways in which stock options could be valued and/or divided, and if requested, can calculate the appreciation over certain time periods of various separate financial contributions to hybrid marital assets.

In the offices of the financial professional, a defined benefit pension plan can be valued, perhaps using an online pension appraiser. The financial professional will explain the choice of neutral or midpoint assumptions for the values of certain variables which must be input. NADA motor vehicle values may be added into the summary of the financial professional. Individuals may obtain a single (not inexpensive) formal business valuation, so as to avoid paying two adversarial hired guns who may skew their results somewhat one way or another.

The financial professional can prepare a useful and trustworthy short summary of the various assets in a high asset case for the mediator and the clients, can analyze the tax consequences, and can describe various options for the division of those assets, taking the wishes of the clients into account. For example, if one client wishes to stay in the former marital home and not pay out half of the equity to the other, appropriate offsets can be suggested and recommended by the financial professional. This summary, and the suggested scenarios for division, can then be used during the mediation sessions. However, if the marital estate is not complex, the assets can be valued and divided during the mediation sessions without an analysis by a third party financial professional using the financial statements.

The clients must be made to clearly understand, however, that if a proper financial analysis is recommended but not undertaken, they are simply agreeing on arbitrary numbers, and must assume the resulting consequences. Their Mediated Agreement will so state. In the Informative Mediation Model it will not be tolerated for one individual to state that he or she has created a spreadsheet of values "equalizing" a division of assets. Any representations of asset values, of an equalization or of offsets must be neutrally verified. Otherwise, the clients are simply "agreeing on a number." It *is* permissible, however, for the clients *to* simply "agree on a number," provided they understand their options, and the fact that that number may not be the number one of their attorneys might argue for if the matter were to be litigated.

Step Four. **The Informative Mediator helps the clients to propose, to evaluate and to agree on options, usually during the second session.**

Once the necessary information has been gathered, including capital gains tax consequences such as for the sale of an investment property, or the tax consequences relating to the sale of the former marital home more than three years after the separation and equity paid out to each, discussion is had over the simple and the difficult topics. Much of the Topics List will often be easily disposed of, such as who will provide health insurance and for how long.

In other areas, the number of choices for resolution may be limited, and after brief discussion agreement will be reached. These areas may include topics such as the division of unreimbursed medical expenses for minor children, and the distribution of the household furnishings.

Then the real work will be done as the mediator calls upon his or her dispute resolution abilities, obtained perhaps through coursework, certification and experience, to assist the parties in reaching agreement in the more difficult areas.

The purpose of this article is to describe the Informative Mediation process, and not to address the ways in which mediators are able to bring clients to resolution. That topic is not addressed herein. I will note, however, that individuals who truly wish to resolve their divorce through nonadversarial mediation will find a way to do so, especially if guided by a competent mediator.

Step Five. **The Informative Mediator writes down the points of agreement, usually during the last session.**

Interim notes may perhaps have been made during the sessions regarding the resolution of discrete subjects, but adjustments may have occurred over the sessions. Once all is resolved, a final session will be devoted to clarifying the agreements reached, and the mediator will make note of these decisions. Some mediators prepare a sort of a "rolling draft" of an Agreement, and update that Agreement after each session, along with billing the clients for the preparation of notes. It may not, however, be necessary to impose such costs upon the clients. Instead, a deposit may simply be requested for the drafting and preparation of the Agreement once almost all, if not all issues have been resolved.

For most topics the mediator's notes need not be lengthy, as the notes will probably refer to certain previously drafted options set forth in the lengthy template of the attorney's form model Agreement. There are only so many ways to describe, for example, the division of extracurricular expenses for the children, and whether that division is aspirational or enforceable.

However, whatever rough notes the mediator has prepared should not be given to the clients, nor to any attorneys down the road should the mediation fail, in order to protect the confidentiality and integrity of this model where attorneys are not directly involved in the mediation process itself. This is important because individuals often take and should feel free to take conciliatory positions in mediation that they would not take in an adversarial process, and should not fear that their words could be used against them later on.

Step Six. **The Informative Mediator explains the meaning of the boilerplate language which will be included in the Mediated Agreement, and the choices within that language, during the last session.**

Boilerplate provisions are important. That is why such provisions are included in agreements of like type.

The clients should know what provisions such as "Waiver of Equitable Distribution" or "Incorporation of Agreement" mean. A reconciliation paragraph should be discussed, as should whether the clients wish to include a Waiver of Estate provision or a Right to Inherit provision. Procedures for future modification should be explained, regarding either modification of the Agreement, or modification of the court order incorporating the Agreement. Whether or not the Agreement should include provisions for attorney's fees for the divorce and for any post-divorce modification proceedings should also be addressed. Boilerplate does not mean unimportant, and it should not be assumed that the same language is appropriate for every Agreement.

Step Seven. **The Informative Mediator explains the actual divorce process to the clients during the last session.**

During the process, discussion will be had regarding which client will file the actual divorce case, and how the attorneys' fees will be paid. The mediator may have another attorney on his or her team in a different law firm willing to file the divorce case at a lower rate, due to the volume of the referrals.

When the court papers are issued after a divorce suit is filed, terms such as "Summons," "twenty-one day time limit," "default judgment," "such other and further relief," "Acceptance of Service/Waiver of Notice," "deposition," "*ore tenus* hearing" and "20-60.3" will pop up. Future concerns of the clients' should be alleviated by an explanation of what is to come, along with explanation of the mechanics of how any retirement order will be submitted for entry and then sent to the administering entity for implementation.

Step Eight. **The Informative Mediator drafts the Agreement.**

The initial draft should be prepared from a standard form each time, and not from Agreements prepared for other clients, so as to avoid tech savvy clients from "mining" the document and discovering the identities of any of the mediator's other clients. The first names of the clients may be used instead of "Husband" and "Wife," and the term "we" may be used instead of "the parties." Much of the "whereas" and "heretofore stated" terminology can be dispensed with.

Step Nine. **The Mediated Agreement is scanned and sent to each client.**

The Agreement should not be sent to the clients as a Word document or other attachment, so as to avoid any temptation on the part of a client to alter the Agreement. The document should be scanned and sent as an attachment which can not be readily revised, such as a .pdf or .tif attachment, with stern orders not to make any changes. The clients should also be instructed to verify that no changes were made before signing.

Usually the finalized Mediated Agreement is complete once drafted, and could be signed by the clients. Four copies should ultimately be signed, so that each client has a fully endorsed copy, one copy can be used for the divorce suit, and one copy should be sent to the mediator for his or her files.

Occasionally, minor bits of information are still missing once the initial draft of the Agreement is prepared, such as the beneficiary amount on an existing term life insurance policy, or one last number to be ascertained. The mediator will have explained that these small items can be discussed by the clients, and one client can email the missing information to the mediator, copying the other client, so as to avoid the mediator entering into a dialogue with just one client. A finalized Agreement can then be sent out.

If the clients wish to suggest revisions, any such revisions should only be made on the mediator's hard drive version of the Agreement. It is not unheard of for the mediator to receive from the clients revisions tracked on a document which had been sent as a scanned attachment, but any revised document should be prepared entirely by the mediator, and not by "accepting" any changes "tracked" on a client's copy.

When the final Agreement is sent to the clients, the letter accompanying the Agreement will state that each client should feel free to have the Agreement reviewed by an individual attorney on his or her own behalf. If the clients do so, and if they each receive no new legal information that they did not receive during the course of the mediation, the Informative Mediator has done his or her job.

Step Ten. **The Informative Mediator prepares any necessary retirement orders, military DD forms and transmittal letters, after receipt of a copy of the signed Mediated Agreement from the clients.**

A copy of the fully endorsed Agreement should always be requested from the clients, so the mediator can verify that the clients did not alter the Agreement on their own. After receipt of the signed Agreement, letters closing the file can be sent.

However, if the Agreement contained language regarding the division of retirement assets, the Informative Mediator may then prepare language for the orders which effectuate the terms of that Agreement. Military and other retirement sections of the Agreement may have been drafted by a retirement benefits specialists after a conference call with the clients. That individual may have emailed the language regarding the retirement benefits to the mediator to be inserted into the Mediated Agreement. That same individual can then prepare the language for the orders, transmittal letters and military DD forms, under the supervision of the attorney mediator, once the Agreement is signed. Or the attorney mediator can prepare the documents and have QDROs preapproved by the Plan Administrators. These orders and documents are then emailed to the clients, who can then forward them on to the divorce attorney to finalize.

Step Eleven. **The Informative Mediator sends closing letters to the clients.**

Once all work is completed, the clients should each be informed in writing that their file is closed.

Conclusion

The process of Informative Mediation well serves clients who wish to resolve the issues regarding the dissolution of their marriages amicably, respectfully and efficiently. Informative Mediation is best conducted by qualified practicing attorney litigators, with highly trained support staff and well-developed teams of supporting specialists familiar with the process. Through Informative Mediation, rational and respectful individuals can privately create specialized and detailed futures for their two-home families, at less overall cost.

Although the above mainly address the use of Informative Mediation to resolve divorce issues, the process of Informative Mediation lends itself well to any other area of dispute, and not only to the mediation of family disputes.

APPENDIX 4

GENERAL LIST OF TOPICS TO BE RESOLVED

1. Custody
   a. physical - sole or shared
   b. legal – sole or joint
   c. if shared physical custody - detailed custodial schedule, or scheduled by agreement
2. Visitation
   a. detailed schedule, or scheduled by agreement
   b. holidays / birthdays / summer / telephonic / travel
3. Child support / direct pay or withholding order / commencement date / arrears
4. Extracurricular activities / camps / holiday gifts / back to school clothes / computers and electronics / tutoring / SAT preparation classes / driver's education classes / car insurance / college application fees / senior year activities
5. College / four years / bachelor's degree / age limit / instate rate cap
6. Alimony
   a. monthly amount, or reserve right to request in the future, or waive the right
   b. if payable - the amount, commencement and due dates, and whether the support is modifiable or nonmodifiable

    c.   if payable - termination upon death, remarriage or cohabitation for a specified duration

    d.   if a reservation, must a significant change in financial circumstances occur for a future request

7. Health coverage / dental / optical / psychological
8. Unreimbursed medical expenses
9. Use of flex fund
10. Life insurance / long-term disability coverage / long-term care coverage

    a.   presently in effect, or to be obtained

    b.   other parent, or the child/ren named directly or in trust as beneficiary

    c.   free choice of trustee, or requirement to name the other parent as trustee

    d.   cash value

11. Former marital home

    a.   exclusive possession

    b.   mortgage payments

    c.   mortgage interest deduction

    d.   utility payments / normal maintenance and repair payments / extraordinary repair costs

    e.   value for buyout or refinance, and by when

    f.   sale if not refinanced by deadline, or short sale

        1)   payment of recommended improvements

        2)   list price / lowering of list price / acceptance of offer of 95% or lower / any further encumbrance prohibited

        3)   division of proceeds

        4)   obligations of estate / death of a party

    g.   contribution to moving expenses

12. Household furnishings and collections / jewelry
13. Investment real estate / timeshares
14. Liquid assets / bank accounts / IRAs / CDs / mutual funds / stocks / stock options / bonds
15. Prepaid tuition plans / 529 educational accounts

16. Division of private, government or military defined benefit retirement pension plans & survivorship rights, or waiver
17. Division of 401K / TSP or other defined contribution retirement accounts & survivorship rights, or waiver
18. Business interests
19. Cars / boats / motorcycles
20. Pets
21. Safe deposit box contents of value
22. Debt / credit cards
23. Filing taxes - refund or liability / exemptions / child care credit / appropriate withholdings
24. Divorce proceedings / determination of date of separation / attorney's fees.
25. Any excluded matters not addressed or resolved
26. Boilerplate language
    a. waiver of claim to estate, or preservation of right to inherit
    b. revocation of any powers of attorney
    c. protection from discharge in bankruptcy of obligations
    d. waiver, or preservation of request for attorneys fees in modification proceedings

Rachel L. Virk, P.C.
46090 Lake Center Plaza, Suite 307
Potomac Falls, VA   20165-5879
Telephone 703 444 3355

www.virk-law.com